An introduction to
psychological tests and scales

An introduction to
psychological tests and scales

Kate Miriam Loewenthal
Royal Holloway College
University of London

UCL
PRESS

First published in 1996 by UCL Press

UCL Press Limited
University College London
Gower Street
London WC1E 6BT

and
1900 Frost Road, Suite 101
Bristol
Pennsylvania 19007-1598

The name of University College London (UCL) is a registered
trade mark used by UCL Press with the consent of the owner.

British Library Cataloguing in Publication Data
A catalogue record for this book is available from the British Library.

Library of Congress Cataloging-in-Publication Data are available.

ISBN:1-85728-405-4

Typeset in Palatino.
Printed and bound by
Page Bros (Norwich) Ltd, England.

Contents

Foreword

It is extremely important for psychologists to have available to them adequate measuring instruments. In several areas of psychology (e.g. social psychology; personality; intelligence) these measuring instruments often take the form of psychological tests and scales. However, most of the authors of books dealing specifically with psychological test construction and evaluation assume that their readers possess great statistical expertise and considerable prior knowledge of psychology. In my experience, this is a dubious assumption to make about academic psychologists, and is wholly unwarranted so far as undergraduate students are concerned!

What Kate Loewenthal has attempted to do (and has succeeded admirably in doing) is to write a book on psychological tests and scales which is accessible and readily comprehensible by those lacking confidence in their understanding of statistics. This accessibility is achieved in part through the clarity and coherence of the writing style. It is also achieved by providing basic guidance on how to construct tests and evaluate their reliability and validity, rather than by focusing on complex and abstract statistical principles.

There are other ways in which Kate Loewenthal's book makes a valuable and distinctive contribution. For example, the number of psychological tests is increasing almost on a daily basis, so that by now there must be several thousand tests available for use by psychologists. However, the key issue of how to find the test that one needs among this myriad of tests is ignored in most other books. Kate Loewenthal provides a number of eminently sensible suggestions as to ways of tracking down any given test.

In sum, Kate Loewenthal, has done an outstanding job of producing a user-friendly account of what is involved in test construction and evaluation. All the stages of finding, choosing, and developing tests and scales are discussed carefully and in detail. As one would expect in this day and age, the book provides detailed instructions on the use of modern statistical software offering reliability and other relevant facilities. The only danger is that Kate Loewenthal may have made the task of test construction too easy for the thousands of readers who will read this book, as a consequence of which the steady trickle of new tests may turn into a downpour! However, that is a risk well worth taking for a book that will rapidly become an indispensable addition to the bookshelves of most psychologists and psychology students.

Michael W. Eysenck

Preface

This book aims to meet the need for an introductory text covering the basics of psychological test and scale construction. It should meet the initial needs of psychology undergraduates and other social scientists in research methods training. Professionals in business and management who wish to develop tests and other instruments for selection, survey or development purposes could use this book to achieve better standards of clarity, reliability and validity.

The development of statistical packages incorporating a facility for measuring test reliability means that the important statistics needed for test development can be fairly easily carried out without having to spend too much time mastering basic statistics. This book is aimed at assisting particularly in the use of computer software facilities for reliability analysis. SPSS-PC (and SPSS-X), SPSS for Windows and CSS are covered. It also outlines the main stages in test and scale construction, which can be applied in developing a test using any statistical package with a reliability facility, or even without a statistical package or computer at all.

There are several books on the market which deal with psychometrics, which is the theory and practice of psychological test construction. Almost all such books are unnecessarily detailed and advanced for introductory undergraduate use, and cannot be recommended to the average undergraduate or others who are seeking to grasp the basic principles of test construction. Although there are good, short research methods handbooks, there is no current basic handbook on psychometrics.

Throughout the book, the traditional terms "test", "scale" and "measure" have been used almost interchangeably. Nowadays the range of psychological states and constructs that are measured is widening the whole time, and the distinction between "test", "scale" and "measure" may be harder to maintain than in the past. "Testing" has traditionally involved comparing performance on the measuring instrument (the test) against standard performances on that instrument. The standard performance ("norm") is the average performance score on the test achieved by people from a specified group. Test scores may be "higher" or "lower" than each other. A psychological or mental test is defined by English & English (1958) as:

a set of standardised or controlled occasions for response presented to an individual with design to elicit a representative sample of his behaviour when meeting a given kind of environmental demand. The occasion for response most often takes the form of a question or similar verbal stimulus.

"Scaling" involves ordering and comparison of performances on the measuring instrument (the scale), without any (absolute) standards necessarily involved. English & English defined a scale as:

a series of test items, tasks or questions, each of which has been given a number or score value on the basis of empirical evidence of their average difficulty for a certain group of people.

Many examples of measures of psychological states, of performances and abilities, of beliefs and attitudes, of cognitions and cognitive styles, of preferences and of personality would be hard to classify firmly as tests or scales.

The terms "person", "subject", "testee" and "respondent" have also been used fairly interchangeably. Each term has its specialist contexts: the subject, traditionally, is a person who participates in a psychological investigation, often an experiment. The testee is the person tested (usually by a psychologist), while the respondent (or interviewee) is the person questioned (usually by a social scientist or survey worker). Readers from different academic or professional backgrounds may prefer one term to others. The American Psychological Association now recommends the term "participant".

This book seeks to convey some basic principles and methods of psychological test and scale construction – not only to those who know they need them, but also to those who should or could be using them but who have not and cannot use them because of their inaccessibility.

Acknowledgements

Many thanks to the following for all kinds of help and support:

My family, especially my husband Tali Loewenthal, and my children (Esther, Leah, Yitzi, Chana-Soro, Moshe, Rivky, Brocha, Freidy, Sholi, Mendy and Zalmy), and the Lubavitcher Rebbe.

Robert West and Jeremy Foster, whose books helped me to get going with SPSS-PC and SPSS for Windows.

SPSS and CSS for being a lot faster than the hand-cranked machines I learned to do statistics with, and SPSS for permission to use copies of SPSS output screens.

Robert West (St George's Hospital Medical School) for his astonishing ability to see both wood and trees simultaneously, and for constructive comments on both in successive drafts of this book.

The following also read and made very helpful comments on drafts of this book: Maxwell Roberts (University of Essex), Brian Evans (Middlesex University), Tony Winefield (University of Adelaide), Melissa Chapman, Kay Eldergill and Rosa Ramos (Royal Holloway University of London).

Rosemary Westley and Mary Atkins and other colleagues (Royal Holloway University of London) for many kind acts of help, particularly chasing up details of tests and related material needed for this book.

The Revd Canon John Brown for allowing me access to his CSS facilities.

Sheila Chown (Emeritus Reader, University of London) who suggested the method of doing reliability analysis without computing facilities described in Appendix 4.

Andrew Carrick for encouragement and support when most needed, which was most of the time.

Chapter 1

What this book does, plus a guide to finding and using existing tests and scales

This book is a step-by-step guide to constructing a reliable and valid measure of reported states of mind or of reported behaviour – a psychological scale, test or measure. It is not a comprehensive manual, but a guide for those who have never attempted test or scale construction before. The book outlines the principles and practices involved. Those most likely to find the book useful are undergraduates in psychology or behavioural science. The book may also be useful to those working in education, health, business and industry. The book is intended as a guide for novices. Some background in statistics and computing would be an advantage though not absolutely essential.

The book will enable you to construct simple self-report measures of psychological constructs, such as beliefs, attitudes, moods, feelings, values, intentions, behaviour, knowledge and skills. Additionally, it should improve your ability to report on the use of, describe and evaluate any existing measure; understand others' reports, descriptions and evaluations; and select a test for use from those already in existence.

It is, however, an introductory book, and deals chiefly with measures of a single psychological factor, using a uniform type of test item enabling scores to be obtained by adding. The procedures involved in standardizing test scores are not covered: use Anastasi (1988), or Kline (1986 or 1993) for coverage of this topic. For more elaborate tests, and for designing tests for use in specialist contexts (such as clinical diagnosis), you would need to use a more specialist book.

Any measure of the type you might want to construct using this book involves assumptions of additivity and interval scaling.

Additivity – the construct measured (for example, depression, or liking for psychologists) will be assessed by asking people to carry out your instructions with regard to a number of *test items*. You might ask, for example, whether certain mood-adjectives were generally applicable to the person, or whether they agreed with certain statements about psychologists. You then add up the answers, to give an overall measure of depression, or liking for psychologists. It is up to you to decide whether additivity seems to be justified. It would not make sense to add the answers to depression items to the answers to items about liking for psychologists, for example.

Interval scaling – once a total score has been obtained by addition, you have to think about whether the "intervals" in your scale are roughly equal. For instance, consider three people scoring say 0, 5 and 10 on a depression measure. To qualify as an interval scale, you have to be fairly confident that the person who scored 10 is more depressed than the person who scored 5, to the *same* extent that the 5-scorer is more depressed than the 0-scorer. If this is difficult to decide, you could comfort yourself with the thought that you may be using Likert's solution, described very shortly. Interval scaling is dealt with much more fully in statistics textbooks; it is mentioned here because most of the statistics that are needed for scale development assume that scores are on an interval scale. Likert (1932) developed a method for scaling using what he called "equal-*appearing* intervals". This involved asking people to say how *much* they agreed or disagreed with test items, or how much the items were applicable to them. For example, how much do you agree with the following? (Underline one of the five alternative answers.)

"I feel pretty cheerful most of the time." Strongly agree / agree somewhat / uncertain / disagree somewhat / strongly disagree.

Answers to items like this are converted to numbers (e.g. +2, +1, 0, -1, -2), and the numbers are added up to give an overall score. The Likert approach is often followed in this book. It should normally be safe to assume that you have at least a rough approximation to an interval scale if you use Likert scaling.

1.1 Features of reliable and valid tests and scales

The points to be covered when presenting a scale are:
- statement of what the scale measures
- justification for the scale

- how the preliminary pool of items was drawn up
- description of the sample used for testing
- descriptive statistics (norms): means, standard deviations and ranges
- reliability statistics
- validity statistics
- the scale.

Appendix 1.1 describes three examples of test and scale presentation.

1.1.1 Statement of what the scale measures

This would not normally be very long. It might be difficult to produce, however, because one is required to formulate and then define the obvious. Try to formulate this statement very early in the development of the scale; preferably it should be the first thing you do.

1.1.2 Justification for the scale

Its background and history, including underlying theory, its uses, and advantages over existing measures should be made clear. You may need to include a rationale for having a scale at all, rather than a single-item measure. For example why you need twenty or thirty questions looking at different facets of belief about prayer, or different symptoms of depressive illness, rather than just one question asking for an indication of favourability to prayer, or extent of depression. Typically, a multi-item measure is needed where there is an underlying central conceptual entity, with a number of facets, which may not be tapped by a single question. In the case of depression, for example, depressed mood, suicide plans, sleep disturbance and so forth do not always go along with each other, and could not be tapped with a single question.

1.1.3 How the preliminary pool of items was drawn up

Give details of the sources used, how (if at all) they were sampled, and any special steps taken to check the wording of the items.

1.1.4 Description of the sample used for testing

Any psychological test or measure should be presented with a description of the group or groups of people who did the test and

3

contributed to the mean score(s). If the test is given to different types of people, we would not necessarily expect their performances to be similar; thus anyone using your test needs to know whether their testee came from the same population as your norming sample, in order to interpret their score(s) in the light of your norms. Any special local or historical circumstances should be noted. For example

126 female New Zealand psychology undergraduates

42 male first-admission schizophrenics

31 children aged 6–9 years described by their teachers as having reading difficulties (20 boys and 11 girls)

535 male British army recruits, tested in the two weeks following the outbreak of the Falklands war.

Mean age and age range should be given where possible, and any details of cultural background that cannot be inferred from knowing the country in which the test was carried out. Ideally, performance of males and females (and any other subgroups) should be examined separately, and if performances differ, means should be presented separately.

1.1.5 Descriptive statistics (norms): means, standard deviations and ranges

These should always be presented. Some published tests do not give these details, and it is annoying for test users to discover that they are not available, because one would generally wish to compare performances of one's testees with norms. Means and ranges are easy to work out. Standard deviations take a while if you are without computer software, but statistical packages are widely available.

The *mean* (average) is the most commonly used measure of central tendency, and is the total of everyone's total scores on the test, divided by the number of people who did the test. Some would prefer to quote an *item mean*, which is the mean score for one item (the scale mean is divided by the number of items). The *standard deviation* is a measure of how much spread there is in the scores (refer to a statistics textbook if you are interested in the details of how it is calculated). The *range* is simply the highest and the lowest score. It is a good idea to show the range actually obtained, and the theoretically possible range if they differ. For example

Mean: 13.45

Standard deviation: 6.74

Range (obtained): 2–24; full range: 0–25.

1.1.6 Reliability statistics

Definition – reliability is consistency. Do different bits of your measure give similar results? If you gave your measure again to the same people would they score similarly? If you gave your measure to similar people, would they score similarly? The British Psychological Society Steering Committee on Test Standards (1992) defines reliability as "the extent to which the outcome of a test remains unaffected by irrelevant variations in the conditions and procedures of testing", and as "consistency of measurement". There are different measures of reliability, and more is said about this below. An unreliable measure is of limited value. If different questions or items on your test give inconsistent results, then you are not assessing anything. This may seem trivial, but a crucial hallmark of a professional test is that you do the work necessary to establish its reliability.

Wording – a test cannot be reliable unless the items are clear and unambiguous. For example, if I want to assess mood, and ask people to indicate which mood-words normally apply to them, I should not normally choose words like "mad" or "favours" in my test because they have different meanings in different cultures ("mad" denotes angry in US English, and insane in British English; "favours" denotes preference and liking to many English-speakers, but in Jamaica, it can mean "resemble"). Thus some knowledge of colloquialisms can be an advantage. Again, this may seem trivial, but it is important to spend time making sure that your items really are about what you intend them to be about. A number of well-known tests fall a little short here.

Correlation – it is important to produce a numerical (statistical) measure of reliability, that is objectively defined, so as to allow comparison between tests. Measures of reliability are usually correlation coefficients. A correlation coefficient can range from 1.0 through 0 down to −1.0, and it is a measure of the strength of association or similarity between two sets of scores obtained by the same people. A correlation coefficient of 1.0 or nearly 1.0 means that the two sets of scores are strongly associated or very similar. A person who obtained a high score on one test or on one occasion got a high score the second time; low scorers on the first set of scores were low scorers on the

5

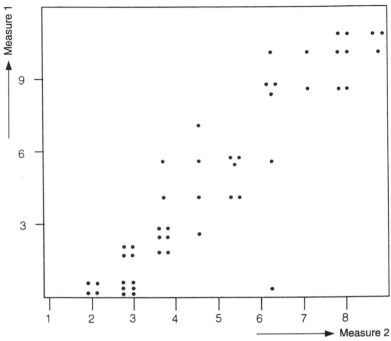

Figure 1.1 A positive correlation (r = +0.868).

second set. A high negative correlation (–1.0 or nearly –1.0) means that the two sets of scores are also strongly associated but the association is negative and high scores in one set of scores go along with *low* scores in the other set, and vice versa. A correlation coefficient of 0 or nearly 0 means that the two sets of scores are not related at all: a high score in one set of scores may be associated with a high score in the other set, or a medium score, or a low score; we just cannot predict anything about scores in the second set from scores in the first set. In evaluating reliability coefficients we are usually looking for high positive values. The statistical significance of a coefficient depends on the size of the coefficient *and* on the size of sample (of people). Figures 1.1–1.3 illustrate what various correlation coefficients indicate about the relationships between two measures.

A high positive correlation means that high values on one measure go along with high values on the other measure (Fig. 1.1). A high negative correlation means that high values on one measure go along

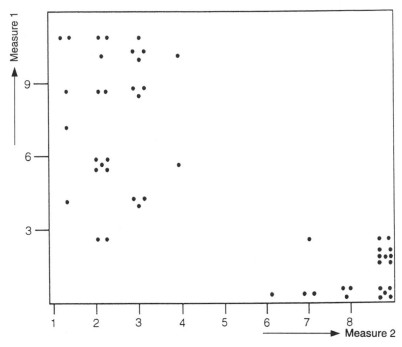

Figure 1.2 A negative correlation (r = –0.804).

with low values on the other measures, and vice versa (Fig. 1.2). A zero or low correlation means that you cannot tell anything about what the value on the second measure is likely to be, from knowing the value on the first measure (Fig. 1.3).

If this is not old news, an example may make things clearer. Let us say I am developing a measure of trust in clinical psychologists, and I give my measure to 50 patients suffering from phobias. A week later I give the same measure to the same 50 patients. A correlation of 0.81 would suggest that high scores the first time generally went with high scores the second time. A correlation of –0.81 (unlikely, but you never know) indicates that high scores the first time went with low scores the second time and vice versa; in other words, most of the patients who said they had some trust the first time, changed their minds, and so did the mistrustful patients. A correlation of, say 0.04 means that scores the first week predicted almost nothing about scores the second week. Only the first result – the fairly high positive

7

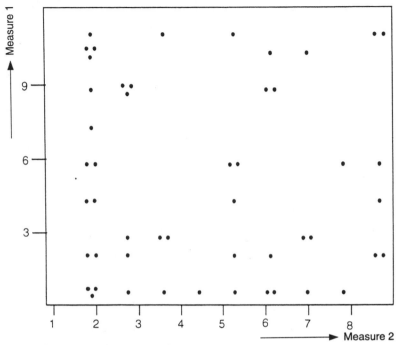

Figure 1.3   A nearly zero correlation (r = –0.018).

correlation of 0.81 – suggests that the test is reliable over time. Kline (1993) suggests that the lowest acceptable figure for the alpha coefficient of reliability would be 0.80. This is rather a tough criterion and the British Psychological Society (1992) suggests that 0.70 might be acceptable. Under some circumstances (see Ch. 4), even 0.60 may be acceptable.

The statistical significance of the correlation is the probability of getting that coefficient by chance, that is, as a result of "sampling error" (your sample is not truly representative of the population it is supposed to represent). A very *low* probability indicates acceptable statistical significance; usually probabilities of less than 0.05 are acceptable, at least for exploratory research and small samples; ideally they should be less than 0.01, especially where sample size is large. Statistical software packages will work out probabilities for you. If you are working without such a package, then statistical tables will have to consulted. In our example, the probability of getting a correlation of 0.76 with a sample of 50 is much less than 0.01, so the result would be considered statistically significant.

Note that the statistical significance of the correlation coefficient tells you nothing about the *direction* and *strength* of the association. This information is given by the coefficient itself.

Forms of reliability assessment

All forms of reliability assessment involve two or more sets of scores from the same group of people, where the scores are supposed to be measures of the same thing. The investigator then calculates a measure of association between the sets of scores – usually a correlation coefficient – while praying hard that the measure of association indicates a good level of agreement between the scores. There are several different ways of assessing reliability, and investigators choose the ones that suit their needs the best. Normally, Cronbach's coefficient alpha is regarded as the most desirable. This coefficient takes into account all the inter-associations between all items in the scale. You may use one of the coefficients generated automatically by a computer package, and the following notes should help you to understand something of what the computer is doing for you. Consult Anastasi (1988) or Kline (1993) for more details on the pros and cons of the different types of reliability.

Test–retest reliability – the same test is given to the same people on two different occasions (this is what happened in the imaginary example of a test assessing trust in clinical psychologists). The correlation between scores on the two occasions is calculated. This form of reliability assessment is not much use if you are assessing transitory states of mind that are easily and rapidly changed (such as mood, and many beliefs, attitudes and intentions).

Split-half reliability – the investigator selects half the items in the test at random, and calculates a total score for that half of the test, and a total score for the other half of the test. The correlation between scores on the two half-tests are then calculated. A variation on split-half reliability is *alternate-forms* reliability, in which two different versions of a test measuring the same thing are given to the same people.

Internal consistency (cohesiveness, item–total correlations) – the investigator calculates the correlation (or other measure of association) between scores on each item of the test, and the total score on the test. This has to be done for each item in the test. Ideally the total should be the total score on the test *minus* the score on the item under

9

consideration. This will yield as many correlations as there are items in the test. It tells you, for each item, how well answers to that item relate to answers to all the other items. It appears lengthy and tedious, but it is the one you probably have to do, as it is the best way to home in on items which are not assessing the same thing as the others. However, the reliability facility on a statistics package (SPSS, CSS/Statistica, SAS) will do the work for you.

Reliability statistics (measures of internal consistency) – tests developed since the 1980s tend to quote computer-generated reliability statistics. The default option (i.e. what it does automatically unless you tell it to do something else) is *Cronbach's alpha (the alpha coefficient of reliability)*. I have always found this coefficient delightfully metaphysical, as it is defined as the estimated correlation of the test with any other test of the same length with similar items (i.e. items from the same item universe) (Kline 1986). If you want to understand how this coefficient is derived and calculated, then you could consult Kline (1993) or Anastasi (1988). The reliability facility on your statistics package will do the computation for you. Alpha should normally be at least 0.70 for reliability to be regarded as satisfactory. Note that unlike a conventional correlation coefficient, it is possible for coefficient alpha to exceed 1.0.

Kuder–Richardson (K-R 20) – this is a coefficient that can be interpreted in exactly the same way as Cronbach's alpha. Your statistics package may calculate it for you automatically in cases where your data are dichotomous and therefore not suitable for ordinary correlation coefficients. Ordinary correlation coefficients can be calculated when people answer each item on a rating scale (say from 0 to 7), or get a score (say from 0 to 20). If they just said "yes" or "no", "agree" or "disagree", then answers would be entered on a database as 0 or 1 (or 1 or 2); the data are said to be dichotomous and the statistics package will calculate K-R 20 instead of Cronbach's alpha. As stated, it can be interpreted in the same way as Cronbach's alpha.

Guttman's coefficients – these and other reliabilities could be calculated. Refer to your statistics package handbook, or to Anastasi (1988) or Kline (1993) if you wish to discover more about them. It may be premature for the beginner at test construction to worry about whether they are needed.

Factor and principal components analyses – the literature on test construction frequently refers to factor analysis. Factor analysis is a way of discovering statistical "factors" among a lot of test items (variables); it is a way of analyzing relations between correlations, so that one can look at relations between all variables rather than just pairs. The first step is the construction of a correlation matrix showing the correlation between each variable and every other variable. West (1991) describes factor analysis as a "technique for finding a small number of underlying dimensions from among a larger number of variables". The final output of a factor analysis includes a list of factors – which are listed in the order in which they contribute to the variance – with "factor loadings" for each variable. These factor loadings show how much every variable contributes to the factor, and they can range from +1.0 to –1.0. The researcher names each factor by examining which variables are most heavily loaded on it.

Factor analysis – you might consider using this if you want to develop a test which is assessing something complicated, in which you suspect more than one underlying factor. A variety of items are needed for assessment, they would not be well associated with each other, and a conventional reliability analysis yields poor results. Factor analysis may also be used when you are unsure what the underlying factors are. When you know what the different factors are, you can write a subscale to assess each, and then examine the reliabilities of each subscale. When you do not know, then factor analysis may tell you. An example of a case for factor analysis was said to be intelligence. Researchers were unsure about the factors involved, and so intelligence tests were constructed by writing many items testing many abilities, and then subjecting performance scores to factor analysis. There has been a certain amount of controversy surrounding the applications of factor analysis to the construction of tests of intelligence, personality and the like.

Principal components analysis – this yields similar results to factor analysis, but gets there by a slightly different route. Instead of looking at the relations between variables, the principal components analysis starts off by looking for factors which explain as much of the variance as possible.

Factor analysis and principal components analysis would be appropriate in the circumstances I have described, and further (conventional) reliability statistics to establish internal consistency would normally be redundant. More sophisticated discussions of the uses of factor analysis in test construction appear for example in Cattell (1946), Eysenck (1952), Anastasi (1988), Cook (1993) and Kline (1993).

If you do decide that factor (or principal components) analysis is for you, then be warned that factor analysis is extremely time-consuming to do by hand: literally weeks or months of work would be involved for a test with more than a few items. Computers, however, will do the work quickly. West (1991) provides a very user-friendly guide. Tabachnick & Fidell (1989) provide a more detailed guide, including a comparison of the factor and principal components analysis facilities on different statistics packages. A brief outline appears in Chapter 4.

Note that some oldish PCs may not have enough hard disc space for these procedures, unless you have only a very small number of items in your test. Extra disk space may have to be installed.

A note on statistics packages – many computer statistics packages exist, some of them tailored specifically for the needs of psychologists. The better-known packages exist in forms suitable for PC or mainframe, IBM or Macintosh, DOS or Windows. Computer software is evolving rapidly and information written now may be out-of-date by the time you read it. At the time of writing, several statistics packages have reliability facilities, as well as more standard facilities for factor analysis and the other statistics referred to in this book. This means that they will compute reliability coefficients, item–total correlations and other statistics relevant to scale construction referred to in this book. Packages which are currently known to do this are SPSS, CSS/Statistica, and SAS. See Appendix 4 for more details.

A useful source of information on statistics packages is *The CTI directory of psychology software* (Trapp & Hammond 1994), which gives a long list of statistics packages. Most of them do not contain reliability facilities, but future editions of the directory could be a place to watch for new developments in reliability software. Tabachnick & Fidell (1989) provide a useful detailed comparison of several statistics packages used in multivariate statistics, but unfortunately their book does not cover test reliability and so no comparison of reliability facilities is given. However, some readers might find the review of software giving other facilities (such as factor analysis) useful.

1.1.7 Validity statistics

Definition (and its relation to reliability) – a valid test is one that measures what it is supposed to measure. The British Psychological Society Steering Committee on Test Standards (1992) defines validity as "the relevance of the scores" and the "extent to which it is possible to make appropriate inferences from the test-scores". Unless a test is reliable it is unlikely to be valid. There are several different types of validity, and you do not have to use them all. You should select one or more methods, depending on your resources and needs.

Content and face validity – content validity is present when the items *are* about what you are measuring, and face validity is present when the items *appear* to be about what you are measuring. For example "Ice-cream is delicious" is a content- and face-valid measure of favourability to ice-cream, whereas "Ice-lollies are delicious" is not (because ice-lollies are not ice-cream). Some researchers think that face validity is not necessary. There are two reasons for this view. One is that you might see a need to be a bit secretive about what you are assessing, to avoid the possibility of testees "faking good" (appearing better than they are). This possibility will discussed again in Chapters 2 and 3, and it raises some serious ethical issues. Another reason for doing without face validity is that if a test is reliable, and valid by other criteria, it may not matter about face validity. The eminent H. J. Eysenck is reported to have said, regarding his measures of neuroticism, "An item can ask whether the moon is made of green cheese, as long as neurotics generally answer one way, and non-neurotics the other". Kline (1986) suggests, however, that subjects may not co-operate unless items appear to have face validity. Kline says that if test instructions are clear and all test items reflect all aspects of the subject being tested, then the test is valid *per se.*

Criterion validity is present when measures on the test differ as predicted according to some criterion. For example two groups of subjects differing by some criterion such as gender, or occupation might respond differently on many tests.

Concurrent validity is shown when your test relates concurrently to some other measure of the same thing. There is always a danger that you can be accused of redundancy, because if you select another test or rating as a criterion against which to validate your test, then you might be asked why your test is necessary at all. The best answer would be along the lines that your new measure is simpler, quicker, more user-friendly, or more useful or cost-effective than the measure against which you have validated your test. For example, psychometric scales may be more reliable than some traditional methods of assessment, such as interviews, where a great deal of training and experience is required to interpret and score the results.

13

Predictive validity is achieved if your test predicts subsequent performance on some criterion. Occupational psychologists and personnel managers, for example, would normally wish that a selection test would predict future work performance.

Construct validity is achieved if you have formulated your test in the context of a theory which makes predictions about behaviour in relation to the test. These predictions would be considerably more elaborate than those expected when looking at criterion or predictive validity. An example would be the predictions made by Eysenck about conditionability and other aspects of behaviour and cognitive functioning according to combinations of scores on the Eysenck Personality Inventory (Eysenck & Eysenck 1975).

There are other facets to test validity, but the ones described are the types most commonly used. For the novice, and for many ordinary test constructors, it is usually a good idea to try to achieve face and content validity, and usually possible to aim for criterion or concurrent validation against some suitable criterion or standard. Predictive validity sounds straightforward on paper, but it involves a prospective research design – research in which the people tested have to be followed-up at a later time. In practice it can be expensive, time-consuming and often very difficult to track down all the people you tested the first time round. However, it may have to be aimed for when developing a test that will be used for selection and therefore must be shown to predict something (Johnson & Blinkhorn 1994). As for construct validity, you need a good theory, a lot of courage, and plenty of time and research funding, none of which come easily.

1.1.8 The scale

Spell out the scale itself, or sample items, plus instructions to subjects. Details of how to go about this appear in Chapter 2. Before you start work, find out if anyone else has already developed a scale measuring what you want to measure.

1.2 Using an existing scale

Clare Bradley once remarked, "Psychologists would rather use each others' toothbrushes than each others' measures". Very often, it seems that one's research problems cannot be resolved by using any existing measure. None of the measures is quite right. But equally often, it seems that there is duplication of effort in test development. Here, for instance, a historian justly complains about the diversity of measures used by eminent social scientists over a nine-year period, in a series of studies to assess anti-semitism (Dawidowicz 1977):

> Unfortunately, no-one thought to draw up a uniform scale that might be applied to all the surveys . . . *Christian Beliefs and Anti-Semitism* (Glock & Stark 1966) used six items for its index; *The Apathetic Majority* (Glock, Selznick & Spaeth 1966), three; *Protest and Prejudice* ((Marx 1967), nine; *The Tenacity of Prejudice* (Selznick & Steinberg 1969), eleven (seven of Marx's items were the same as Selznick and Steinberg's). *Wayward Shepherds* (Stark, Foster, Glock & Quinley 1971) changed the ground rules and formulated an index that differed from the one used in *Christian Beliefs and Anti-Semitism* (its predecessor). The anti-semitism index in *Adolescent Prejudice* (Glock, Wuthnow, Piliavin & Spencer 1975) consisted of eight items, a few similar to, but none identical with, the eleven-item index in Selznick and Steinberg. Of the various authors, Marx alone employed "positive" items – that is, items favourable toward Jews.

This section describes how to go about discovering whether you are in danger of wasting time by re-inventing a psychometric wheel that is already rolling along beautifully. It is better to try to avoid causing complaints like the one just quoted.

1.2.1 Finding the scale

There are a number of steps involved in identifying a suitable test. Once you have found one, some of the later stages in the search can be omitted.

First, make a note of possible key words covering the content of what you want to assess, and make a note of key features the measure should have, such as type of reliability, type of validity, type of item, and so on. The American Psychological Association has produced a very comprehensive list of features (summarized in Appendix 1.2). Briefer guides include the British Psychological Society Steering Committee on Test Standards' very useful booklet, *Psychological testing: a guide* (1992), which outlines the features of good psychological measurements and the safeguards to be employed in using them.

15

Another useful booklet is produced by the Institute of Personnel Management (IPM), called the *IPM code on psychological testing* (1993). Appendix 1.2 gives more details.

Secondly, Appendix 1.6 provides a short review of some commonly used tests and scales. You could glance at this first, and then decide whether you need to conduct a more thorough search.

Thirdly, the Mental Health Portfolio is an interesting new development pioneered by the National Foundation for Educational Research (NFER). Institutions may buy a set of tests and then photocopy and use them freely within the institution. A list of the measures included in the Mental Health Portfolio appears in Appendix 1.4. This portfolio is primarily of interest to those working in the clinical context, but many of the tests have applications in occupational, counselling, health care and other settings. Other portfolios are in preparation.

Fourthly, investigate any stock of tests held in your place of work or study, and ask likely colleagues or acquaintances if they have or know of anything suitable.

Fifthly, search one or more databases, such as *PsychLit* or *Psychological abstracts*. *PsychLit* is a CD-ROM database of abstracts of psychological articles published since 1972 and of books and book chapters published since 1987. There are other databases of the same type covering medicine, education and the social sciences which could be useful: consult a university library information service. *PsychLit* is the most likely database for discovery of less well known psychological measures. It gives the same sort of information – author, title and publication details, and an abstract – as *Psychological abstracts*. The simplest way to use *PsychLit* is to ask it to search for the topic(s) and/or author(s) that you want. It will tell you how many abstracts it has found with the word(s) you told it to look for. If you give it a "big" topic, like depression or memory, there will be too many to look through so you should try to narrow it down by telling it look for, say, depression and chronic and adolescents, or memory and episodic – or whatever your focus is. Ideally you want everything that has been published on your topic without having to wade through too much irrelevant material. When you find something that is appropriate, make a note of the details and track down the publication in your library, or another library, or via an inter-library loan service. *PsychLit* will print or download bibliographic details, and you can include the abstract if desired. Be warned, however, that *PsychLit* is not the last word. You may not find everything in the field you are looking for, as there are a number of smaller circulation, specialist journals, specialist books and booklets which are not covered. Unpublished conference presentations and privately circulated reports are also not included. This may not matter for some purposes, but if you need to be thorough or scholarly, or if you are working in a very specialist field, you may have to set up personal links. Internet may also be useful.

Psychological abstracts has an index of authors and topics covered by most of the articles and books published in academic psychology. You may prefer to use a computer databank (e.g. *PsychLit*) for more modern publications, but *Psychological abstracts* is still a useful resource for older tests and for literature about their use. Remember that many tests are (and were) published in academic journals rather than by commercial publishers. To use *Psychological abstracts*, look up the topic(s) you want in the enormous alphabetical subject index, and record the numbers given. These are the abstract numbers of the relevant articles and books. You can look up these abstracts in *Psychological abstracts*, and then if you want more details, track down the original publication in your library, another library, or via an interlibrary loan service.

Sixthly, consult test reviews. Buros' *Mental measurements yearbook* (the latest at the time of writing is the eleventh, plus a 1994 update) is a valuable resource for learning about many tests, though it may not cover the more specialized or unpublished. It includes details of price and distributor, and some tests are reviewed in more depth, giving details of reliability and validation work, and views on uses and applications. Note that each yearbook is an *update* on information published in earlier yearbooks, so in consulting Buros you will find yourself referred to earlier yearbooks for some information on (reviews of) older tests. Thus access to a set going back, say, twenty or thirty years is desirable. The publishers are Gryphon Press, Highland Park, 220 Montgomery Street, New Jersey, USA. The UK distributors are Academic and University Publishers Group, 1 Gower Street, London WC1E 6HA (tel: 0171 580 3994).

Useful briefer guides include Bartram et al.'s (1990 plus updates) *Review of psychometric tests for assessment in vocational training*, which is a useful resource if you are looking for tests in the occupational, selection and assessment areas. Swetland et al. (1983) describe assessments for use in psychology, business and education, but do not give information on reliability and validity.

17

Seventhly, there are a number of publishers of psychological tests, and their catalogues could be consulted if you have been unable to locate a measure that can be used free of charge. Some test publishers are listed in Appendix 1.3, the *Mental measurements yearbook* publishes a full list. When buying from a test publisher, remember that you have to buy not only as many copies of the test as you need, but also a test manual and possibly a scoring key. Delivery may take time, especially if the test comes from an overseas distributor. Test publishers operate restrictions concerning who may purchase and use their tests (see also Sections 1.2.2 and 1.2.3). Buying a test takes time and money. Ensure that it assesses what you want it to, and that it meets the requirements of a good test. If you have never seen what the test looks like, you can ask the test distributor for a sample copy before you commit yourself to spending a large sum of money.

Finally, personal links with others working on topics similar to yours (networking) may be necessary. This can be achieved by going to conferences, writing to authors of work in the area you are interested in, or using E-mail or fax to contact them.

1.2.2 Copyright

The copyright of published tests is usually owned by the publishers. Anyone who photocopies a test (or who reproduces it by other means) is effectively stealing, and is certainly breaking the law. Some institutions and individuals have been successfully prosecuted for violating copyright, particularly by the use of photocopying. So if a test is published commercially, you should buy it, not photocopy it. However, tests published in academic journals may be used, although you should get permission from the author and/or the journal concerned. Academic authors are usually happy to discover that someone is interested in using their test.

1.2.3 Test user restrictions

Some tests require special training: the famous (or notorious) Rorschach (ink-blot) test used for describing personality and psychopathology is one example. Another is the Myers–Briggs Type Indicator (Myers & McCaulley 1985), popular among occupational psychologists, which assesses personality according to the Jungian typology and for which some claims have been made regarding its predictive validity in occupational performance (Ryckman 1993).

Other tests may not need such specialist training, but professional training and qualifications are required by the test distributors before the test can be obtained. In the UK, Chartered Psychologist status is needed for the use of many tests. A Chartered Psychologist is (briefly) a psychology graduate who has undergone approved postgraduate training and/or qualifications. If you need to find out more details, contact the British Psychological Society, St Andrews House, 48 Princess Road East, Leicester LE1 7DR (tel: 01162 549568).

The British Psychological Society is setting up certificates of competence in occupational testing (Bartram 1993; British Psychological Society 1994) further details of which are given in Appendix 1.5. These certificates are designed for non-psychologists who need to use psychological tests in their professional work. They would normally be redundant for those who hold a psychology degree of a type which would give graduate basis for registration with the British Psychological Society. Some tests may be used under the supervision of a qualified user. Other tests require no special qualifications for use. Test distributors should and do ensure that tests are purchased only by or for qualified users.

1.2.4 Offensiveness

Many scales and tests can be seen as threatening, intrusive or offensive by some people, even when there were no apparent problems when they were first developed. For example, some traditional or religious groups of people are likely to find questions to do with sex-related matters offensive, not regarding them as a matter for public discussion or record. Many measures of clinical states (such as depression and anxiety) may be seen as threatening and frightening. Using a measure in which the first item is "I feel inadequate most of the time" could alarm many people, and some may refuse to do the test at all. Some people may feel that test results reflect on their abilities, or depict them in some crucial way. One can never be sure which issues are going to touch an individual most deeply, but you may have a good idea what might be crucial for the kind of people you are going to be testing.

All the safeguards to do with opting-out, anonymity and other ethical issues described in Chapters 2 and 3 may help to protect people to an extent, but if you have really offended people, these may not be enough. Always be on the look-out for the sensitivities of the people you are testing, and be prepared to abandon tests and items that could cause distress.

1.2.5 Pros and cons of using an existing scale

In summary, you might choose to use an existing scale if it
- can be obtained quickly enough
- can be obtained cheaply enough (preferably free of charge)
- does not require an expensive, time-consuming training
- does not exclude you from using it
- does not contain dated or meaningless language
- measures what you want measured
- is reliable
- is valid
- provides relevant norms
- enables useful comparisons, for example with other groups of people, or with people in conditions different from those you are testing
- does not offend or distress people.

If existing measures fail on any of those points, you would be right to develop your own; the biggest loss is probably the opportunity to make meaningful comparisons.

1.3 Summary

This book explains how to construct a reliable, valid measure of reported states of mind or behaviour. In this chapter, the criteria of "good" psychometric measures were set out, notably reliability and validity. Finally, there was a guide to finding and using existing tests.

Chapter 2

Writing

This chapter describes the first stage of scale development – writing your preliminary scale. This first version will be longer than the final scale; be prepared to produce more items than you really want to include in the final version. All the items should be as "good" as you can make them at this stage, but some may have to be discarded because they do not meet all the necessary criteria.

2.1 Defining what you want to measure

The first important step is to work out and write down exactly what you want to measure. Show your proposal to all concerned with the work, assess and respond to their comments. You need to be clear about what you are assessing in order to ensure face and content validity. You need to think about whether you are assessing a single psychological factor, or more than one. Often, what seems like a single mood, set of beliefs or other psychological factor, may prove to be more complicated. For example

Anxious mood
Self-rated religiosity
Liking for chocolate
Musical preference

These all look straightforward, but there are problems with all of them, and similar problems are likely to occur with anything you want to assess. For example, with anxious mood, you would need to decide whether you want to distinguish anxiety from depression and other distress states, which may co-occur with anxiety. Otherwise you may finish up assessing forms of distress other than anxiety – without intending to, and finding effects which are not truly the result of "pure" anxiety when you look for performance or behaviour which might be associated with anxiety. You also need to decide whether to define anxiety as the presence of distress states only, or whether you want to look for the absence of positive states such as calmness.

With self-rated religiosity, you would need to decide whether to distinguish between internal religious feelings and experiences, and outward observances, such as affiliation and practice. Are you going to look at one religion or denomination only? Are you going to concern yourself with so-called religious orientation (whether the person claims to be genuinely devout, and/or religious for social or other extrinsic reasons)?

With liking for chocolate, you would need to think about whether to concern yourself with different forms of chocolate, with the question of chocolate addiction versus liking for the taste, with the roles played by chocolate-eating in the person's life, and so on.

With musical preference, you would need to decide whether to look at liking for music in general, and different uses of music (listening, performance, therapy, dance, etc.), as well as different types of music.

These are just a few of the kinds of problems. When such problems arise, do not panic. If it all seems straightforward, then something is probably wrong. If a research design seems initially complex and full of problems, you are probably on the right lines. The general procedure is to read up what you can about the area of investigation. This should reveal likely problems and indicate how others have tackled them. You must decide on your own solutions, and be prepared to justify them.

2.2 Collecting items

2.2.1 How many items?

Now decide approximately how many items you want in your final measure. Too few items may not produce a reliable measure: a notorious feature of the reliability coefficient alpha is that it tends to be too low to meet acceptability criteria when there are few items on a scale. Too many items, and the people you want to test may feel daunted by the length of the scale, and there may be repetitiousness.

Useful scales may contain as few as three or four items, but it is a bit risky to aim for such a short measure. Something between six and fifteen items should be enough for assessing a single "factor". To ensure this, you should start with between ten and thirty items. If, however, you have several subscales, you will need to keep each subscale as short as possible so as not finish up with a monster with fifty or even a hundred or more items. No matter how interesting the topic, most people will lose enthusiasm before they have finished. As a rough guide, tests with more than one subscale could have between three and fifteen items per subscale in the final test, and you need to generate about twice as many for preliminary testing. If you have to have very short subscales, you may wish to try a reliability index other than alpha, or content yourself with low alphas.

2.2.2 Sources of items

Your sources of items will normally be discourse and text, which may be produced from *brainstorming* sessions, where you and others may sit and write items, or informal *conversations*, which may generate ideas. *Open-ended qualitative interviews* are a more systematic method of ensuring that you cover the ground. For further information consult a handbook such as Brenner et al. (1985) or McCracken (1988). You will need to construct an interview schedule: allowing respondents to speak freely is not a free-for-all as far as the investigator is concerned. You will need to ensure that you use listening and prompting skills correctly, and avoid evaluative, over-directive or interpretative comments; an interview is not a conversation. You should record the methods used to sample or select interviewees, and you need to observe basic research ethics, including confidentiality and making clear to interviewees that they can withdraw at any time. For group discussion (focus group) sessions, many of the techniques are similar to those used in interviewing; consult a guide on the use of focus groups, such as Higginbotham & Cox (1979), Morgan (1988) or Krueger (1994). Published or unpublished texts may be used as a source of brief quotes or ideas which you can use as a basis for your items. With published texts make sure you do not violate copyright restrictions, notably by quoting too heavily from any published work. Quotation of more than 50 words may need the consent of the copyright holder. With unpublished texts you need to ensure that you are not violating confidentiality.

2.2.3 Checking the items

Having generated or collected a large pool of potential items, items need to be checked to ensure that they meet the following criteria. Try to get at least one other opinion.

Face validity (see Ch. 5) – does the item appear to be about what you want to assess? For example "I love ice-lollies" has no true face validity on a scale assessing favourability to ice-cream. (You may have decided *not* to aim for face validity: see Section 1.1.7)

Content validity (see Ch. 5) – *is* the item about what you want to assess?

Lack of ambiguity – "I often feel mad" might be unambiguous to North Americans, but may be ambiguous or misleading to speakers of British English. Other examples could be quoted. Try to check items with one or more people from the group(s) you are targeting.

Not double-barrelled – it is surprising how often one can finish up with double-barrelled statements, sometimes as a result of trying to achieve clarity; the respondent does not know which part to respond to: for example "People in authority often do irresponsible or dangerous things".

Reversing meaning – if you are assessing attitudes to or beliefs about a particular issue, it is important to create some items which are contrary to the attitude or belief under investigation, to combat the possibility that you may be assessing yea-saying (which is the tendency to agree with any statement, especially if it comes from an authoritative or official-looking source, and which can affect answers quite considerably).

Social desirability – this is something you may not be able to do much about when creating items, but once an item is written, think about whether it might be socially desirable to answer in one way or another; if this possibility exists, you would need to assess social desirability effects. For example, some people may not want to admit to feeling depressed, or angry, or to holding certain beliefs. Alternatively, they may exaggerate the extent to which they feel happy, or hold certain beliefs. A social-desirability measure may be used (e.g. the Marlowe–Crowne Social Desirability Inventory – Crown & Marlowe 1960). If you are concerned, you may be able to set your mind at rest by showing that your measure is not associated with social desirability. If there is an association, you may be able to weed out those items which are strongly associated with social desirability.

Offensiveness – if you are investigating sensitive issues, you need to be particularly careful not to cause offence. Always be alert for this, as you should avoid upsetting people, for both ethical and pragmatic reasons.

It is important to get at least one other viewpoint in addition to your own. When you have been closely concerned with creating items, you need a fresh mind to check most of the above criteria. Eliminate items or rewrite until you have items which have face/content validity (assuming that you do not wish to avoid these forms of validity), which are unambiguous (and not double-barrelled), and unlikely to cause offence. Where appropriate, make sure that some of your items are "anti-", and think about whether social desirability effects are possible, taking action as suggested above if necessary.

2.3 Producing the preliminary questionnaire/test

When you are ready to produce a preliminary version of the questionnaire or scale, use word-processing or, where appropriate, a graphics package to produce an attractive version. There are a few more points to bear in mind at this stage.

2.3.1 Anonymity, ethics and the law

There are a number of ethical and legal points to bear in mind when collecting answers to your scale items. Some guidelines from relevant professional and academic organizations appear in Appendices 1.2 and 3. The suggestions below should ensure that you do not break any laws or offend anyone. If you are working with special groups such as children, medical patients, disturbed or disabled people, further precautions will have to be taken: these will include getting permission and advice from a research ethics committee.

Ethically and legally, you may not collect and store information about people in a way that could abuse their trust in giving you information about how they think or feel. If you are collecting information on one occasion only, anonymity should be guaranteed. Do not, therefore, ask for people's names. It is a good idea to point out explicitly that names should not be written on your forms/questionnaires.

If, however, you want to follow-up your subjects on a second or subsequent occasion, you will almost certainly have to identify them, and collect details of how to locate them again. Follow these rules:

1. Record identification details (name, address, phone number) on a separate sheet of paper from other information given by the subject; do not enter it on to the same database as the research information given by the subjects.
2. Make clear to subjects that this information will be destroyed as soon as the follow-up is completed.
3. Assign each subject a code number, which will enable you to line up the follow-up information with the first lot of information.
4. Destroy the identification information as soon as follow-up is completed.
5. Do not look at the names of who said what, even if the names mean nothing to you. This will protect anonymity if you should ever come across those individuals again.

As well as guaranteeing anonymity, you need to include a verbal or written assurance that the person giving the information is free to withdraw at any time, and does not need to give reasons for their withdrawal. Some older tests and questionnaires have stern commands such as "Answer all the questions. Do not leave any out". It is better to avoid this kind of language. If it is in the *subject's* interest to answer all the questions – for instance if you are trying to get a performance score, or a diagnosis of some kind – you can include something like "Try to answer all the questions" or "A better/more meaningful result will be obtained if you attempt to answer all the questions". If it is only in the interests of the investigation to get all the answers, it is better to add an explicit statement such as "If you prefer to omit any question for any reason, please feel free to do so".

2.3.2 Demographic and other data: deciding what is needed

As well as wanting responses to your items, you need to be clear about what other information you need. Decide what you need and work out a format for information such as age, gender, occupation, religion, and so on. Do not ask for any unnecessary information, and be careful not to cause offence.

2.3.3 Response formats

There are several ways in which you might ask for responses to the items in your scale. It is important to use the *same* format for items

Table 2.1 An example of a Likert-type response format.

Mark the statement which shows how you generally feel				
Strongly agree	Agree somewhat	Uncertain or neutral	Disagree somewhat	Strongly disagree
It is important to pray when you need help				

which are going to be added to each other. If this is not possible you would have to adopt methods of standardization beyond the scope of this book.

In *Likert scales*, people are asked to say how much they agree/disagree, or how much they think a description applies to them; five or seven points are the most popular. You have a choice about how people are asked to give their response using the Likert format. Table 2.1 shows one example.

In other formats, people are asked to circle a preferred response, or to write numbers to indicate the extent of agreement/applicability of the statement.

A simpler yes/no or agree/disagree format may be more suitable in some cases, for example if your scale is part of a survey, and you want to know what per cent of those asked agreed or disagreed with each item. If it is important to get your scale completed quickly, this format can give very rapid completion. You simply instruct people to look through and tick those items which they agree with/think apply to them/think are true.

In a *forced-choice* format people are asked to select which of two or more statements or descriptions they prefer or feel is more appropriate. For example:

Circle A or B, whichever you feel is most true of your feelings:
A – It is important to pray when you need help
B – Regular contemplative prayer is important

Appendix 1.1 gives more examples of this forced-choice format.

In a *visual analogue scale* (VAS), there is a horizontal line across the page, on which people are asked to place a mark to indicate their feelings or beliefs (Fig. 4.1 in Ch. 4 illustrates an example). Responses to these scales are time-consuming to score, because you have to measure them. However, some subjects like the freedom of being able to place their responses in any position, rather than being forced into categories.

27

In some tests and scales, answers can be *weighted*. This is not essential, and if you are a novice, it may be better not to attempt this. Weighting is carried out by multiplying the response to each item by a number which represents the importance of that response in relation to the construct you are measuring. One method of weighting is to carry out a factor analysis and compute a factor score for each item (see Ch. 4). Another, based on Thurstone (1931), is to ask people ("judges") to assign weightings which are ratings of the relevance or importance of the item to the construct you are assessing, and to take the mean of these. If you suspect that item weighting is needed, consult a more advanced handbook on test construction (e.g. Anastasi 1988).

2.3.4 A suggested format

Table 2.2 shows an example of how the beginning of a questionnaire might look. This example starts with questions on demographic factors (age, gender, etc.), and sometimes it is better to start with the more "interesting" questions of the scale itself. Sometimes, however, it may be startling or threatening to plunge straight to the point: only you can decide whether to put the demographic questions before or after the scale. Try to set things out so that subjects are clear about how to give the information you want, and so that they can do this easily.

Being open about the purposes of any questionnaire or test seems the simplest way to maximize the chances of getting honest answers; this, in turn, will improve the psychometric properties of your test (reliability and validity). Some psychologists have suggested that there are occasions when total honesty is not necessarily the best policy. If there seem to be good reasons to practise deception, and conceal the true aims of your questions, you should bear in mind the need to de-brief subjects after they have completed your questionnaire or test. This involves clarifying the true purpose of the questionnaire or test; explaining why this could not be made clear at the beginning; and offering subjects the chance to withdraw the information they have given you. To ensure and demonstrate that you have done this clearly and consistently, it is a good idea to set the de-briefing out in writing.

Finally, try to lay out the questionnaire so as to be as economical as possible with paper. (This saves forests and photocopying.)

Table 2.2 An example of a simple questionnaire and scale format.

Questionnaire on prayer

We are studying people's views on the uses of prayer.
Your answers to the following questions would be very helpful. Your answers will be confidential and anonymous, identified only by a code number. You need not answer any questions that you would prefer to leave unanswered.

Thank you.

Date_____

Your age_____

Male/female_____

Current marital status (circle one)

  married engaged single cohabiting divorced widowed separated

Number of children, if any_____

Their ages_____

Your occupation_____

If married, your spouse's occupation_____

Do you belong to any church, mosque or synagogue?_____

If yes, which?_____

How often do you attend?(circle one)

  daily weekly monthly occasionally never

How often do you pray? (circle one)

  daily weekly monthly occasionally never

How often do you study religious texts? (Circle one)

  daily weekly monthly occasionally never

Write a number next to each of the following statements to show how much you agree with it:

5 = strongly agree
4 = agree somewhat
3 = uncertain or neutral
2 = disagree somewhat
1 = strongly disagree

1. It is important to pray when you need help.
2. Prayer is a waste of time.
3. Praying gives comfort.
4. It is foolish to believe that prayers get answered.
5. Regular contemplative prayer is important.
6. People who get inspired by prayer are kidding themselves.
7. Prayer puts things in perspective.
8. There are better routes to understanding life's mysteries than praying.

2.4 Summary

This chapter described the importance of being clear about what you want to measure, methods of collecting and checking items, response formats, and the other steps you need to go through to produce a first questionnaire. Important ethical considerations were mentioned.

Chapter 3

Testing

Having put together a preliminary questionnaire or test, you are ready to go. The next step is one of the most daunting and also one of the most interesting of the whole process of investigation: finding out what people really think and say in response to your questionnaire. But – which people?

If you are a student and simply wish to collect as many answers as possible in a short time, then you can run around your college or university begging other students to do your test. But this is not a random sample of anything or anybody, so do not say that it is (some students do). It is perfectly all right to test students, but when you report your work, say that you used a convenience sample (see Section 3.1.3) of students, and give some description of what type of students, and descriptive statistics of at least age and gender.

You may wish or need to test other types of people. If so, here are some points to bear in mind.

3.1 Deciding on a sample and reducing sample bias

First, decide what your target population is. You might want as representative a sample as possible of British or North American or Japanese adults. Or you may be interested in some special group such as women who have just given birth to their first child, professional musicians, adults suffering from a particular anxiety disorder, or users of a particular type of shampoo. You may want to compare people from your target population with one or more comparison groups, who differ from the target group in one or more crucial respects. For example, you might want to compare women who have

31

just given birth to their first child with men who have just become fathers for the first time, or with women with no children, or with women who have just given birth to their second child, or with women with one child who was born say more than six months ago. When comparing two or more groups, it is important to try to keep all characteristics constant except the one whose effects or correlates you are interested in studying.

In all cases, you decide on a target population, and then select people from it in such as way as to maximize the chances that the people who do your test are as representative as possible of the target population. Volunteers are not truly representative, so it is better to try and get a list or source of at least some of the population, sample randomly from that and approach those selected.

3.1.1 Methods of sampling: random and quasi-random

First, obtain a list or source of subjects. Any list or source is likely to exclude some of your target population. For example, sampling from a telephone directory excludes those in households with no telephone, homeless people, those who have not yet been listed, and those with ex-directory numbers. Sampling from hospital records to select women who have just given birth to their first child will exclude those who gave birth elsewhere. Try to get the best list you can. You may need to get special permission to get access to the list you need, and hospitals and some other institutions have ethical committees who must approve every piece of proposed investigation to be done on people contacted via the institution. All this can take time and effort to organize, and can sometimes be abortive.

Random sampling means using random numbers to select those to be approached. The random numbers can be computer-generated, taken from a table of random numbers, or you can write numbers on pieces of paper, put them in a container, give them all a good shake and pick out however many you are going to approach. Most books on research methods and statistics have random number tables.

Quasi-random sampling involves counting your list and taking one name in every five (or ten, or whatever). Unless you suspect that this will produce a systematic bias, this method can be used if you want something a bit simpler than true random sampling.

3.1.2 Methods of sampling: quotas or target group

Sometimes you can try to achieve representativeness by taking quotas of people from particular categories, in the proportions in which they are reported to occur in that population (or in the proportions that you need for your research design). For example you might take equal numbers of men and women, and equal numbers of socio-economic groups ABC1 and C2DE. This is sometimes called stratified sampling, and it can be done randomly within quotas.

Where you are simply aiming to fill a quota, or to recruit a certain number from a target group, you are not committed to random sampling. You are more likely to get sample bias if you do not use random sampling, but if you are interested in looking at differences between two groups in relation to some independent or classification variable (gender, occupation, use of particular types of shampoos, and so forth) this may not really matter so much (see Section 3.1.3 for possible methods). You should try to ensure that your quotas or target groups have been equated for factors that may affect what you are assessing, such as age, general health, intellectual functioning and so forth.

3.1.3 Methods of sampling: convenience and snowball

These are two non-random methods which may be used to fill quotas or target groups. There are other methods (see e.g. Coolican 1990) but these are the two most straightforward.

Convenience sampling means testing whoever it is convenient to test. Sometimes this is called opportunity sampling. Sample bias is more likely than if random methods are used, but if you are interested in the effects or correlates of a particular independent variable, then random sampling may be less important than if you wanted to find out the general level of response to your questions. For example if you were investigating fear of death or liking for ice-cream, you would try to get random sample from the general population if you were interested in "absolute" levels of (or proportions of people with) fear of death or liking for ice-cream. If, however, you were interested in the effects of a particular religious belief on fear of death, or of hot weather on liking for ice-cream then random sampling does not matter so much because you are looking at *relative* levels – for example, whether stronger belief in life after death is associated with *lower* levels of fear of death, or hot weather associated with *higher* levels of liking for ice-cream than is cold weather. You obviously need to consider whether the independent variable you are looking at (belief in life after death, hot weather) may be confounded with other variables. Especially if you are using convenience sampling, keep a watchful eye on factors like age which might affect what you are assessing. Try to ensure that your groups are comparable on such variables (or use appropriate statistics, as described in Section 5.2.6).

Snowball sampling is useful when you want to fill quotas or target groups, and there is no ready supply of suitable people. You might want to locate people with a particular (but rare) disability or set of beliefs, or a particular ethnic group. You locate one or two suitable people who are willing to do your test, and ask them if they can suggest one or two others who might be willing to help, and then those people are asked for more names, and so on. In the shampoo-user case, you might ask if the person knows any friends who use this type of shampoo. This method of recruitment is pleasant to use, because you may already have an "introduction"; you can ask the people giving you each name whether they mind their name being mentioned when you approach their acquaintance. Usually it is very effective. Of course it does not give a random sample.

More detailed discussions of sampling methodology may be found for example in Kish (1965), Coolican (1990) or de Vaus (1993).

3.1.4 Response rates

If you are trying to ensure minimum sample bias, you have to be able to demonstrate that no bias was introduced at the stage of recruitment by large numbers of people declining to do your questionnaire.

Keep a record of *first*, how many people could not be contacted (for example you wrote to them and they did not reply; then you tried phoning, say five times, but there was no answer; or someone answered the phone, but not the person you were seeking); *secondly*, how many people you contacted but who declined to participate (*x* in the formula below); and *thirdly* how many people you contacted and who agreed to participate (*y* in the formula below); if they started but did not finish, you can still count them as participants, unless they said they wanted their record destroyed. Missing answers can be entered as missing values on the computer, and you will still have some usable data from those people who did something but did not complete.

To calculate response rate, you could normally disregard the first category. Response rate is the percentage of participants, out of the total number of people who were asked to participate:

$$\text{Response rate} = \frac{y}{x+y} \times 100\%$$

where x and y are the numbers of people recorded under the second and third categories.

Published research usually reports response rates of at least 70 per cent, with rates well over 90 per cent in many investigations. Occasionally there may be special groups or other circumstances involving low response rates of the order of 50 per cent or less. When rates are below about 70 per cent you have to consider whether there is any sample bias among those agreeing to participate. This can be difficult, of course, because it could be difficult to find out anything about people who could not or would not answer any of your questions. But you can look for over-representation of certain groups of people among those who did participate. You might find, for instance, that there are more retired or unemployed people in your sample than you might expect from what is known about the proportions of these groups in the population you are studying.

When reporting your findings, report response rates; if they were low, say what you can about how the sample appeared to be biased and how this might have affected responses to your questionnaire or test.

3.1.5 Sample size and statistical power

It is often thought good to aim for large samples. This is not always so (Coolican 1990) because averaging what large numbers of people have said or done may conceal important individual or group differences.

There are two principal reasons for trying to get a large sample: first, *reduced sample bias*, because sample bias is generally reduced in larger samples, and second, *improved statistical power*, because if you are looking for statistically significant differences or associations, the power of the statistical test to detect such differences is related to sample size. Statistical power is also related to the size of the effects you have got (or hope to get), and to what you have decided is an acceptable level of statistical significance. Cohen (1988) explains all, while Cohen (1992) explains all you probably need to know for most

Table 3.1   Minimum sample sizes for some basic research designs (adapted from Cohen 1992).

The sample sizes given below apply where a medium effect size is expected, alpha is 0.05, and the power specification is 0.80.

Test	Minimum sample size
Mean difference	64
Correlation	85
χ^2 with 1 d.f.	87
Anova with 3 groups	52 per group
Anova with 4 groups	45 per group

purposes. Statistical power is stated by Cohen (1992) to be the probability that a given investigation will lead to statistically significant results. This helpful guide explains that normally a power specification of 0.80 would be made, and one would normally expect a medium effect size; if then alpha (acceptable significance level) is set at 0.05, Table 3.1 shows the minimum sample sizes required (note that in the context of discussions of statistical power, "alpha" has nothing to do with the reliability coefficient of that name).

You would need to consult Cohen (1988 or 1992) for required sample sizes where effect size and alpha differ from those described above, and for further research designs and statistical tests. The figures above are for some common scenarios. Brewin (1993) has pointed out that if the principles of power analysis are applied – and there are increasing calls for this to be done – the trend should be towards simpler research designs, with smaller numbers of groups (and independent variables), in order to ensure adequate sample sizes.

3.2 Recruiting

You now have to persuade people to do your questionnaire or test. Some suggested methods are described below.

3.2.1 Methods of recruiting

Direct approach involves approaching a potential subject, saying something along the following lines:

Good morning/afternoon. My name is . . . , and I am (a student at . . ./working for . . . I/we are conducting a study of (topic) and I/we would be very grateful if you spare a few minutes to (answer a few questions/look at this questionnaire and see if you would be willing to answer the questions).

People may be approached by door-to-door calling (carry some identification and credentials) or in the street, provided you choose a safe area and time of day. If you are a student, your campus is probably safest.

Mailshots produce notoriously poor response rates (normally well under 50 per cent).

Telephoning strangers ("cold-calling") can also be unproductive; a better method may be to send a letter setting out the purpose of your investigation, and explaining that you are going to telephone shortly to ask if the person is willing to help. When you phone, you will have saved yourself a lot of time explaining the basics, and if the answer is to be "no", at least it is usually given quickly.

Use of institutions – it is always tempting to consider this, since you may have access to large numbers of the type of people you are looking for, and it may even be possible to test groups of people together. However, institutions must protect their members, and you will usually have to go through lengthy administrative processes before you get permission to approach people through institutions. Some (especially hospitals and other health service institutions) will have their own ethical committees. Be prepared to submit a written proposal, explaining and justifying your research and explaining why you need to approach people through the institution. You will also need to submit a copy of your questionnaire, and explain who you are, and you may have to meet one or more managers. Be prepared for a long wait – sometimes several months – and a possible rejection. Do not, therefore, rely on one institution. If you have contacts, this can be useful, as personal acquaintance may reassure those responsible that you are trustworthy, that you are doing something useful, and will behave responsibly. If your work will produce something that is useful to the institution, that is an advantage.

3.2.2 Ethical issues

Respect is the most important underlying principle: respect for the right to opt in or opt out, respect for privacy and respect for confidentiality. It is also important to express *thanks* for help, and to *explain* how the help that has been given will be used and will be useful.

People recruited to do your questionnaire or test should always be invited (not coerced) to participate. Always make clear that they should omit any question they prefer not to answer, and are free to stop at any time *without giving a reason*. Testing conditions must be *private* (ensure that the subject's answers cannot be overseen or overheard) and undisturbed. Subjects should know that their answers are to be treated *confidentially and anonymously*. Feedback may be given, but consult the guidelines in Appendix 3.3, which call for a delicate combination of honesty and tact. Appendices 1.2 and 3 offer other ethical considerations and further suggestions about how to put ethical principles into practice.

3.3 Testing

Decide whether you want people to write their answers, or deliver them verbally. Writing is better with literate adults, and where there are no obvious difficulties. Remember to provide writing instruments, a firm surface to write on, and private, quiet, undisturbed surroundings.

If you have a short questionnaire which you are delivering in various localities, or you are testing children, or adults who might have some difficulty with reading or writing, you will need to collect spoken answers. Short answers can be written down, but if you have any open-ended questions you may need to use a tape-recorder. Some people do not like this; obviously you need to get permission to record. Make sure you promise to turn the machine off immediately they ask for this. You can also reassure people that they will probably stop noticing the recorder after a couple of minutes.

Sometimes there might be good reason to record speech or behaviour – whether in writing or otherwise – *without the person's awareness*. This is not very likely in normal questionnaire and assessment work, but it might arise with a very short measure. Make sure that the subjects know what you have done, and have given permission for you to use your records of what they have said or done. Appendix 3 offers further guidelines on testing and feedback.

3.3.1 Group or individual testing?

Groups of people are often hard to come by, but testing groups usually yields results more quickly than testing individuals. You should try to make sure that everyone has understood the instructions, and is feeling happy about co-operating. If you fail on either point, you may get too many spoilt questionnaires; if they are completely spoilt you will have to record them as non-responses rather than incomplete.

3.3.2 Thanking, de-briefing and follow-up

Remember to thank your respondents, and to add any further explanations that are necessary. Answer all questions as well as you can. Occasionally people may ask for details of the results. In that case you will have to ask for their name and address, and you can send either a copy of your report, provided it is not too technical or confidential, or a summary of your results. Do not forget to add a note of thanks for their help, and give your name and address (for example in case more details are required).

3.4 Summary

This chapter described the points you need to be careful about in selecting and approaching subjects, in order to ensure a sample which is as representative as possible of the group(s) tested. The chapter also described means of protecting the wellbeing of the people participating in the development of your measure.

Chapter 4

Coding, database and reliability analysis

When the questionnaires and tests are completed by as many people as you need, your data are coded (where this is necessary) and entered on to a computer database, ensuring that the records of each person are not named. You work out which are the best, most reliable, items in your scale and discard the rest. You will then have a "final" scale consisting of these items, on which you can work out a final total for each subject, and produce descriptive statistics for this final scale (norms). This scale will then be ready for validation work.

For each stage I shall describe what has to be done, and explain how to do it. Appendix 4 gives examples of what to do with and without SPSS or CSS.

4.1 Coding, scoring and data entry

4.1.1 Coding data

Responses which do not need coding
Most answers that are already in numerical form, such as age, and the answers to scale items, if these were given in a numerical form (e.g. +2, +1, 0, −1, −2, or 5, 4, 3, 2, 1) do not need coding. You do not need to do anything except enter them as they are on to the computer database. Answers with a yes/no response format can also be entered directly on to the computer database: 1 for a "yes" and 0 for a "no". Similarly, if you were using a checklist format, answers to each item would be entered as 1 where an item had been checked, and 0 where it had not. (Strictly speaking, this *is* coding, but it is so simple that you can enter the coded responses straight on to the computer database.)

Table 4.1 Examples of items which do not need coding.

Type of item	Example	Example of answer	What you enter on on database
Item requiring numerical answer	Age	23	23
Likert-type scale item	Liking for this chocolate (1 = very low, 2 = quite low, 3 = moderate 4 = quite high 5 = very high)	4	4
Yes/no or checklist	Mark words that apply to this chocolate:		
	sweet	✗	1
	creamy	✗	1
	bitter		0
	spicy		0
Forced-choice	Which one would you choose for your next snack:		
	this chocolate	✗	1
	another chocolate		0
	another snack		0

Forced-choice format answers, where your subjects have to select one of several alternatives, can be entered as 1 for items selected, and 0 for those not selected. Later, you can compute scores from this information.

Table 4.1 shows examples of items that do not need coding and which can be entered directly on to the computer database. Remember that some databases require that a number is entered to represent any missing values. Alphabetical information needs special treatment beyond the scope of this book. Therefore, as just indicated, translate "yes" into "1" and "no" into "0".

Information which needs coding
Other information will need to be coded so that you (or the computer) can do statistics. To speed things up and reduce errors, many researchers pre-code their questionnaires by placing the appropriate code next to each response option (see Table 4.2). The codes are put in an out-of-the-way column, perhaps with a heading "Office use only".

Table 4.2 Example of a pre-coded questionnaire item.

How much do you like this chocolate?

(tick one answer)	Office use only
Very much	5
Quite a lot	4
Moderately	3
Not very much	2
Not at all	1

There are three main types of information that need coding. First, if your subjects answered your scale items by checking one of several ordered responses, instead of writing a number (for example, "strongly agree, agree somewhat, neutral, disagree somewhat or strongly disagree"), you translate the answers into a simple ordered number scale. In this case, it could be +2, +1, 0, –1, –2, or 5, 4, 3, 2, 1. It does not matter which, as long as you *consistently* apply the *same* scale to *each* item. You can use this procedure for a scale with any number of points: 3, 5, 7, 9 and 11 are the most common. You might wonder what to do about *"reverse-meaning"* items, where agreeing with such items suggests an "opposite" set of beliefs or attitudes or feelings, compared to agreeing with other items. In such cases, you still give the same "score" to "strongly agree" and so forth. However, later, you will be able to tell the computer to reverse the scoring of such items.

Secondly, a *visual analogue scale* (VAS) is a horizontal line across the page, on which people are asked to place a mark to indicate their feelings or beliefs. Figure 4.1 shows an example. (As stated in Ch. 2, responses to these scales are more time-consuming to score than other types of response, so consider whether it is worthwhile to use this method.) The example suggests that the person tested perceived the chocolate as sweet and creamy, bland and rather boring. With a VAS, you score the answers by measuring the distance in centimetres or millimetres from the left-hand end of the line. This number is entered on to the database. When describing variables assessed on a VAS, use the word on the *right*-hand side of the scale.

Thirdly, if you have asked for background socio-demographic data from your subjects, some of these (such as gender, occupation or group membership) will need to be translated into an appropriate number scale. You should be aware of what type of number scale

On each line, place a mark to indicate how this chocolate tastes:
For example, if you think the chocolate tastes very pleasant, put a mark very near the word pleasant, like this:

Pleasant _X_____ Unpleasant

If you think the chocolate is quite unpleasant, place a mark quite near the word unpleasant:

Pleasant _____X_ Unpleasant

If you think the chocolate is neither pleasant nor unpleasant put a mark near the middle:

Pleasant _____X_____ Unpleasant

Mark each line to show what you thought of the chocolate:

Sweet __X_____ Bitter
Boring _____X_____ Exciting
Sharp _____X_ Creamy
Bland _____X_____ Tasty

Figure 4.1 Visual analogue scales (VASs), with instructions.

(interval, ordinal or categorical) you are using because this will affect the kinds of statistics that are appropriate. Consult Appendices 4.1 and 4.2 if you feel doubtful.

4.1.2 Scoring: when to calculate total scores

If you are using a computer, there is normally no point in calculating people's total scores on the scale at this point. Assuming you are going to do a reliability analysis, the computer software will calculate the totals it needs. Following reliability analysis, you will discard some of the items on the scale, and then you will be able to calculate total scores on your refined scale. You will be able to do this using the computer. However, it is a good idea to reverse the scoring of any "reverse-meaning" items as soon as possible, and to save these reversed scores. This chapter and Appendix 4 describe how to do this.

4.1.3 Making a database

This can be done using almost any modern word-processing, spreadsheet or statistics package. If you are making the database using software which is different from the one you will be using for statistics, make sure that your statistics package can use the database, or that you can make an export file. Export files should be possible with most modern software. Some packages offer an export option, and a choice of what "language" you want your data translated into. Other export options, more humbly but adequately, offer to translate your file into DOS or ASCII. DOS/ASCII files can be understood or imported by most statistics packages (Appendix 4.3 gives an example of how to make an export file from a Word Perfect database).

If you have access to a *spreadsheet* format for data entry – *use it!* It is much easier and more accurate than the more "primitive" method of simply writing data on to the screen. SPSS for Windows and CSS include a spreadsheet for data entry, or you can use any spreadsheet with an export facility.

Entering the data
1. Start with an ID number for each subject (person who did your test).
2. Enter the coded responses to your questions, including the answers to the main part of the questionnaire, which can be entered just as they are, if they are in numerical form. Data should normally be in numerical form; seek advice if you think you have to enter alphabetical information.
3. *Either* use tabs to position each piece of data, *or* leave a single space between each piece of data, *or* enter each piece of data in a new space if using a spreadsheet.
4. Start a new line/row for each subject. If you are not using a spreadsheet (e.g. you are using DOS or word-processing), don't worry if you have so many data for each subject that the entry for each subject occupies more than one row. This doesn't matter. But you should still start each subject's data with a new row.
5. Make sure that you have equal numbers of pieces of data for each subject. Unless you are using a spreadsheet which will accept "blanks", if any answer is missing, you will still need to give it a number which you will use for all *missing values*. Decide on a number which is not otherwise going to be used (–1, 9 and 99 are

popular for missing values), and put that whenever an answer is missing.

6. If you get stuck, consult West (1991), Foster (1993) or another book on computing for social scientists or psychologists, or ask a friend with relevant computing experience, or a computing adviser.

7. Remember to save the database as you go along, especially if you have a big database. Also, make a back-up copy on a floppy disc. Use the same filename each time you save, over-writing the older version.

4.1.4 Checking for accuracy

Once the database is complete, you should carry out some checks for accuracy, before you can start statistical analyses. If you have not used a spreadsheet, probably the most important database check is to *ensure that you have the correct number of pieces of data for each subject.* It is relatively simple to do. Ask for a list of one variable – best to choose subjects' identification (ID) numbers. If you have the right number of pieces of data for each subject, then the ID numbers should appear on the screen in order. If you have made a mistake, then you will get one or more ID numbers in order, then a messy string of bits of data. For example

1
2
3
4
0
9.7
34
2
3.01
etc.

The last ID number to appear in order is the number of the subject for whom you entered too few or too many pieces of data. In the above example, it was the person with ID number 4. Go back to your original database and correct the problem. Then try listing the ID numbers again until you get a string of ID numbers in order. Note that this check is unnecessary for those using a spreadsheet.

You should check over your database for errors. It is usually easier to do this from a print-out of the data. This applies to those using spreadsheets, as well as to those making other forms of database. The safest way to carry out this checking is to work in pairs. One member of the pair has the original data, and the other looks at the computer database. One person reads out the data and the other person shouts out when they spot a mis-match. Correct all mistakes on the computer database, and save the corrected version.

4.1.5 Saving the database

You can now enter commands which
- if necessary give the values used for *missing data*
- *recode* any negatively worded (reverse-meaning) items
- (compute total scores if you need them at this point: see Sections 4.1.2 and 4.3)
- *save your data file*.

(Appendix 4 provides instructions.)

4.2 Selecting reliable items

Instructions for computing reliability appear in Appendix 4.

4.2.1 The first reliability statistics

Section 1.1.6 defined the main types of reliability. A statistics package with a reliability facility will normally give you one reliability statistic (Cronbach's alpha) by default, and you can specify others if needed. Appendix 4.8 offers suggestions about how to proceed if you have no reliability facility in your statistics package, and if you have no statistics package.

If you want to understand more fully what the different reliability options mean, Chapter 1 gives an outline. You should also study the statistics package handbook, combined with a handbook of test construction such as Kline (1993) or Anastasi (1988).

The first reliability statistic to look at is Cronbach's alpha, a widely used reliability coefficient. This is the estimated correlation of the test with any other test of the same length with similar items (i.e. items from the same item universe). It is possible for alpha (unlike other correlation coefficients) to exceed 1, so don't be alarmed if this happens. The square root of alpha is the estimated correlation of the test with true scores.

What are the *criteria of acceptability for reliability coefficients*? Kline (1993) recommends a minimum of 0.80. The British Psychological Society's Committee on Test Standards suggests that 0.70 might be acceptable. If you have a scale with a small number of items, you are not likely to get reliability coefficients as high as this, and you may consider using a slightly lower criterion (of about 0.6) *if* (and only if):

- there is good evidence for validity
- there are good theoretical and/or practical reasons for the scale
- the scale is short (less than about ten items).

Many test constructors develop tests which are long and *repetitious*; these features ensure high reliability coefficients. This is not very good practice: subjects may get bored or suspicious if the same sort of question is asked over and over again, and improving internal consistency by these dubious means will not improve validity. It is better to settle for an alpha of around 0.60, given the conditions listed above.

However, there are legitimate steps you can take to improve the reliability of your scale. The first thing to try is "cleaning up" your scale by weeding out those items which are lowering the internal cohesiveness. Section 4.2.2 describes how this can be done.

The K-R 20 (Kuder–Richardson 20) is a special case of the alpha coefficient, for items that have been dichotomously scored. You should not have to do anything to get this statistic. Your reliability facility should produce it automatically when there are only two values on a variable, instead of Cronbach's alpha. It can be interpreted in the same way.

Your reliability facility can compute other reliability coefficients (split-half, for example – see your menus or handbook for the full range of commands), but normally Cronbach's alpha, probably the default option, should be used. This is said to be regarded by Cronbach (1951) and Nunnally (1978) as the most important index of test reliability. The split-half reliability coefficient could be useful if you have only a small number of items in a scale or subscale (in this situation you are unlikely to get a sufficiently high alpha).

If you think there might be some subscales within your overall scale, you can get alphas for the subscales by optional subcommands. For instance, in our prayer example the scale was written with two kinds of items: those valuing prayer as a way of getting what one wants (instrumental), and those looking at prayer as a form of strengthening or inspiring communication with the divine (inspirational). You could look at the reliabilities of these subscales. Appendix 4 gives instructions.

If your test/scale used a *forced-choice* format, you may need to use the subscale facilities for getting the reliabilities of the different subscales covered by the choices offered to the subjects. For example, if you wanted to find out people's habitual distress mode, you might present a number of items like this:

> When someone pushes in front of me in line, I feel on the whole:
> angry
> tense
> worthless
> If I get disappointing news, such as doing worse than expected in a test, I feel on the whole:
> depressed
> worried
> annoyed

In this example, people are asked to choose *one* answer. There are three hypothetical subscales (anger, depression and anxiety) and the score on each is the number of times a relevant emotion is chosen. You would need to look at reliabilities for all three subscales. However, if your forced-choice alternatives are just "rubbish" apart from the one you are interested in, there is obviously no need to look at subscale reliabilities. For example, in tests of knowledge or ability, the alternatives to the correct answer do not form separate subscales, as in:

> Churchill was:
> a World War II General
> a British Prime Minister
> the place of a famous battle
> Pearl Harbor was:
> the place of a famous battle
> a singer
> a jewellery shop

The score here is the number of correct items endorsed and since there is no rhyme or reason in the alternatives, you do not treat them as subscales.

4.2.2 Improving the reliability of the scale

There are five courses of action, and if you are lucky you may not have to adopt more than one or two. If you are very unlucky, all five will have to be followed.

First, you may have high reliability coefficients, and might decide to keep your scale (and any subscales) as it stands. No action is needed.

Secondly, if your reliabilities are low, you must look at each item to see how it relates to all the others. This is worth doing even with high reliability if you want to improve the reliability still further. This is done by looking at item–total correlations. A reliability facility can give item–total correlations between each item and the total of the other items in the scale (thus the total is not contaminated by the contribution of the item in question). This indexes the *cohesiveness* of the scale. Appendix 4.8 suggests how to examine scale cohesiveness without a reliability facility. If you have subscales you should look at correlations between each item from each subscale with the relevant subscale totals (the reliability facility will do this). You reject items with unsatisfactory item–total correlations.

You may find that your reliability facility will tell you the effect on the reliability coefficient of removing any given item. This information will tell a similar story to the item–total correlation, and you may find it simpler and clearer to go straight for this information as a way of improving your scale. You can overlook the item–total correlations, or glance at them to check that they confirm that you have made the right decisions: items with low item–total correlations should be the ones whose removal leads to the biggest improvement in the reliability coefficient.

Thirdly, if the number of items in your scale (or subscale) is small, alpha is likely to be low even if they are quite strongly associated with each other. Try calculating split-half reliability, which involves the following steps:
1. divide the items randomly into two groups of equal size
2. calculate a total for each of these half-scales
3. calculate the correlation coefficient between these half-scales.
A reliability facility will do all this for you without your having to go through the above steps.

Fourthly, a scale may have poor overall cohesiveness, and this may be because there are subscales (factors) which you had not suspected.

Try factor or principal components analysis (see Section 4.4). If the results make sense and produce a factor (or factors) on which items with high loadings relate to the construct(s) you are assessing, then items with high loadings (0.3 or 0.4 and above) are retained. Note that this method may give you two or more factors, suggesting the existence of two or more subscales. For each subscale, retain and score only those items with high loadings on the relevant factor. Note that if an item has a negative loading, its score will have to be reversed.

Finally, the last and saddest resort is to salvage any items that seem worthwhile, write some more items, and start testing again. However, as discussed, avoid the all-too-common failing of generating a lot of repetitious items.

4.3 Descriptive statistics (norms) for the final scale

You define your final scale by listing only those items with satisfactory item–total correlation, and obtain Cronbach's alpha (or other reliability coefficient), the number of cases, mean, range and variance of the final scale and of any subscales.

Some would prefer to divide the scale mean by the number of items in the scale, to give an *item mean*. The advantage of this is that if you have to vary the number of items in the scale, then comparisons with the item mean would still make some sense.

If you have decided to use *item weightings*, then answers to each item must be multiplied by the relevant weighting before the mean score on the scale is determined.

The production of *standardized scores* is beyond the scope of this book; Anastasi (1988) or Kline (1993) should be followed if these are desired.

4.4 Summary of steps for data entry and reliability

1. Code data where needed.
2. Enter data.
3. Check data.
4. Enter values of any missing data if necessary.
5. Recode where necessary (for "reverse-meaning" items).
6. Save data file.

7. Compute reliability coefficient (usually Cronbach's alpha) for scale and any subscales. If satisfactory, you can go straight to stage 9.
8. If this is unsatisfactory (less than 0.70–0.80) examine item–total correlations (scale cohesiveness).
9. Remove items with unsatisfactory item–total correlations.
10. Produce descriptive statistics (norms) for final scale, containing only those items with satisfactory item–total correlations: number of cases, mean, range and variance (or standard deviation), and reliability coefficients.

If this fails to produce a scale with a satisfactory reliability coefficient, you could attempt factor or principal components analyses. When describing any scale with dubious reliability, you should state that the scale does not meet criteria for reliability.

4.5 Factor and principal components analyses

If you are developing a scale for professional use or major research purposes, some psychometricians would regard factor analysis as an essential procedure in the construction of psychological scales and tests. However, if you have obtained satisfactory reliability and/or you are not applying the scale in a major way, you could omit this step.

The underlying theory is a specialist aspect of statistics, and there is a good deal of controversy surrounding the applications of factor analysis. See Section 1.1.6 for reference to relevant discussions.

For those taking first steps in scale construction, you could consider using factor analysis if you thought there were several factors in your scale, but you were not sure which items were contributing to them. Factor analysis will tell you the answers to these questions, and so, too will principal components analysis. Section 1.1.6 gives a brief description of factor and principal components analyses and explains the difference between them. It is suggested that principal components analysis may give clearer answers than factor analysis. Appendix 4 offers brief instructions for carrying out factor and principal components analyses.

If you do a factor analysis, you need to examine which items load heavily on each factor. Common criteria are, normally, loadings of 0.4 and above, or loadings of 0.3 and above where there are few or no high loadings, for example, and where it would make sense in naming the factors to include items with slightly lower loadings. Name the factor according to the items that load heavily on it: make a list, and look for a common feature. Note that *negative* loadings indicate that the item is negatively associated with the factor.

You do not have to accept and use all the factors; as a rough guide, the first 1–4 factors will probably account for quite a lot of variance each, and after that there may be a sudden drop. A typical scenario would be for factor 1 to account for about 13 per cent, factor 2 about 8 per cent, and then factors 3 and 4 to account only for a mere 3 per cent or 4 per cent each. Look for such a drop, and use it as a cut-off point in accepting which factors to use. Accept only factors accounting for, say, about 8 per cent or more of the variance. Accept only factors that make sense in terms of the constructs you are assessing. Of course, a reasonable amount of variance should be accounted for. This means that if a factor accounts for a lot of variance, and it does not make sense or is not of interest to you, then you don't have to use it.

In our hypothetical example in the appendices, the item–total correlations, alphas and factor analysis are all telling more or less the same story, which is that once item 6 goes, there is a reasonably consistent full scale, and two subscales.

If you do a factor analysis you may want to consider whether to use *item weightings*. Weighting the items means that an item with high weighting contributes more to the score than an item with low weighting. The main advantage of weighting is that it could give a more sensitive scale, possibly with improved validity. The main disadvantage is that calculation of scale totals and norming data is more complicated and time-consuming. Responses to each item have to multiplied by the item weighting (of course this is normally done by the computer). You could certainly consider using weighted scores if you find the results of your validity analyses are disappointing. There are several ways of developing item weightings: factor loadings can be used as item weightings, or the factor analysis facility on a statistics package will calculate factor scores (consult your statistics package manual). If you are thinking of using item weightings, a more advanced manual on test construction should be consulted.

A simpler application of factor analysis, which has some of the advantages of item weighting without the disadvantages, is to *use the factor loadings as criteria* for retaining items in the scale(s). Decide whether to use a loading of 0.3 or 0.4 as a cut-off, and accept only items with this loading or higher in your scale(s). This may improve the sensitivity and reliability of your scale, without the extra computational labour of item weightings. However, unless you had an undiscovered subscale structure embedded in your scale, which only factor analysis could reveal, this method is unlikely to give much better results than a reliability (item) analysis.

If the results of factor analysis look useful, and you need more information than is provided in this book, you could consult West (1991) for a more detailed guide to doing factor analysis (this covers SPSS-PC and -X only, but is a useful introduction). Tabachnick & Fidell (1989) present a much more detailed account of factor analysis, including a comparison of the relevant statistics packages.

4.6 Summary

This chapter described how to get a final, reliable scale from the pool of items that your subjects have responded to. This involved coding your questionnaire, making a database and using a reliability analysis to see how strongly each item, in turn, relates to all the other items in the scale (or subscale). Those that do not relate well are removed, and the result should be a consistent, reliable scale. Factor and principal components analyses were briefly outlined, and item weighting was mentioned.

Chapter 5

The final scale and its validation

5.1 Descriptive statistics (norms)

Your scale is almost complete. You have
- a list of the items to be included
- range, mean(s) and standard deviations (or variances, which are the square of the standard deviations); these are the descriptive statistics proper, or norms
- a description of the sample(s) associated with each mean
- reliability statistics
- established content and possibly face validity.

The preceding chapters have described how to do all of this, and so far the achievement of two types of validity (content and face) have been discussed. These are achieved at the point of developing the initial scale (see Ch. 2 especially Section 2.2.3). The rest of this chapter is concerned with other forms of validity.

5.2 Validity

Several methods of exploring validity are suggested in this section. You do not have to assess the validity of your scale on all these criteria, but it is usually advisable to achieve content (and probably face) validity, and/or at least one other type of validity.

5.2.1 Criterion validity

Criterion validity means comparing performances on your test or scale with some criterion. For example, comparing the performances of two or more different groups of people on your test, when you could hypothesize that they should perform differently. This can be tested by carrying out an *unrelated t-test* if two groups are being compared, or a *one-way analysis of variance* (anova) if more than two groups are compared. At this point you need to compute subjects' total scores on your new scale, which you may not have done yet.

A *t-test* would specify the grouping variable as the independent variable or group; the dependent variable would be scores on your final scale. If you had predicted the *direction* of the difference, a one-tailed t-test is appropriate; if not, then the two-tailed t value should be taken. For example, in the prayer example, religious affiliation is the grouping (independent) variable. We would expect that the religiously affiliated would have higher scores on the prayer scale than the non-affiliated, so a one-tailed t-test would be appropriate. Appendix 5 shows how to carry out a t-test using different versions of SPSS, and CSS. Section 5.2.4 describes the use of analysis of variance in validity testing.

When describing the results of your criterion validity testing, you would say something like:

> One measure of criterion validity was tested and found to be satisfactory. Comparison was made of the total prayer scores of the non-affiliated (n = 32) with the affiliated (n = 48) in a convenience sample of 50 female and 30 male British undergraduate students aged 19–46 (mean age 22.5). The mean score for the affiliated sample was 15.17, and mean for the unaffiliated sample was 11.5, t = 4.97, d.f. = 78, one-tailed p = 0.000.

When describing the results of criterion validity testing describe:
- the characteristics of those tested (age, gender, etc.)
- how they were sampled
- the means associated with the groups
- the value of t, degrees of freedom, and probability.

5.2.2 Concurrent validity; comparison with existing tests

Concurrent validity means looking at the performance of your subjects on one or more other methods of assessing what your test is assessing. This is potentially quite an embarrassing situation because if there is another test assessing what your scale is assessing, you have to demonstrate why your scale is necessary. This can be done by establishing that, by comparison with the standard (comparison) test, your scale is superior on one or more of the following features:

- meets reliability criteria as well or better
- is (on other criteria of validity) as valid or has better validity
- is as quick or quicker to administer
- can be used on as wide or wider range of people
- is preferable on some other attribute: for example your test might be more interesting or less threatening than the existing standard test, and this is associated with higher completion rates.

Your test should be no worse than the standard test on any of the above criteria, and it should be an improvement in at least one respect.

If there is a standard test measuring something similar to yours, and it is reliable and valid, then you can examine correlations between scores on the two tests. If there is a significant association, then your test has concurrent validity. The two tests obviously have to be completed by the same people – preferably on the same occasion (otherwise any lack of association between the two might be due to different circumstances at the time of testing).

If your subjects did the standard test on a later occasion, you can add the results to your database. Appendix 5 describes how this may be done using SPSS or CSS. You then *correlate* scores on the two tests. Methods of doing this in SPSS and CSS are described in Appendix 5. The correlation(s) should of course be in the expected direction, and statistically significant.

In presenting the results of concurrent validity testing, you would say something like:

> One form of concurrent validity was tested and found to be satisfactory. A sample of 80 British undergraduates (50 female and 30 male, aged 19–46, mean age 22.5) completed the prayer scale and Smith's (1932) attitudes to prayer scale. The (Pearson) correlation was $r = 0.452$, $p < 0.001$.
>
> The new prayer scale is suggested as a rapid and convenient alternative to Smith's scale, which is much longer, having 50 items, some of which appear archaic.

5.2.3 Content and face validity

Content and face validity should be done when you are writing the scale, by seeing if one or more independent judges agree that your items appear to be or are about what you are trying to measure. Items that judges are doubtful about should be discarded.

5.2.4 Predictive validity

The other methods of determining validity are often more difficult to deal with. Predictive validity is achieved if your test predicts behaviour occurring *after* testing. The main problem is the worry and time involved in following up the people who did your test, as described in Section 1.1.7. Nevertheless you will have to consider getting such data, if you are trying to create a test that will be useful only if it can predict performance. Sometimes follow-up data may come your way quite easily. Such data can be added to your database (as described in Appendices 4 and 5).

If the data consist of scores on some measure, you can correlate scores on your test with these performance scores (see Appendix 5 for methods of carrying out a correlation using SPSS or CSS). If the performance measure is binary (for example, did the people succeed or fail on something, do or not do something?) the simplest way to look at associations is to do a t-test using the binary performance measure as a grouping variable, and scores on your test as the dependent variable (see Section 5.2.1 and Appendix 5). If the performance measure is categorical, but there are more than two categories, then a one-way analysis of variance could be done, using the performance measure as a grouping variable. Appendix 5 describes how to do this in SPSS and CSS.

To present the results of an analysis of variance, you can present an analysis of variance table if there was a fairly complex research design involving two or more grouping variables, and/or a mixed analysis of variance involving within-subjects and between-subjects effects. In a case with only one grouping variable, an anova table is not necessary; you need to describe only one F ratio, and the results can be presented by quoting the F ratio, the two relevant figures for degrees of freedom, and the probability. For example

> Significant differences in prayer scores went with later religious-group-joining: $F_2 77 = 51.55$, $p < 0.001$. Subjects were 80 British undergraduates (50 female and 30 male, aged 19–46, mean age 22.5). Those who joined a campus religious group scored significantly higher than those who did not. Post-hoc

comparisons using Scheffe's test showed no significant differences between those joining the two religious groups (Anglicans mean = 5.69; New Christians mean = 5.89); both these groups scored significantly higher than those not joining a religious group (mean = 2.77).

5.2.5 Construct validity

This is obtained when what you are measuring relates to other factors in ways that were predicted by the theory underlying the development of your test. If such a possibility arises, you should be able to carry out tests of associations between variables using correlation, unrelated t-test, analysis of variance or methods of partialling out spurious effects, described in this chapter and in the appendices to this chapter.

5.2.6 Confounded variables

Sometimes two or more variables may be confounded with each other (they co-vary) and this can affect the results of validity testing. "True" relationships can be obscured. For example, if we found that students who believed in the efficacy of prayer were more likely to join religious groups on campus, we might begin to worry about whether this was a true effect if we noticed an age difference between those joining religious groups and those not joining. Perhaps it is really age that is related to beliefs about prayer, and not religious group membership as such? Or perhaps both factors are related to beliefs about prayer?

If you suspect that there are confounded variables in your data, select the appropriate analysis from Table 5.1.

All these tests will express the "true" association between the dependent (outcome) variable and, in turn, each of the independent (predictor) variables which have been entered into the analysis, whilst taking out the "spurious" contribution of the other independent variables in the analysis.

Appendix 5.7 provides brief further details, but if you wish to use any of these methods of analysis you may need to consult a textbook such as Tabachnick & Fidell (1989), a guide such as West (1991) and/ or your statistics software manual.

Table 5.1 Selecting the right analysis when there may be confounded variables.

	Independent (predictor) variable(s): categorical	Independent (predictor) variable(s): continuous
Dependent (outcome) variable: categorical	Loglinear analysis (hiloglinear)	Logistic regression*
Dependent (outcome) variable: continuous	Analysis of covariance (ancova)**	Multiple regression analysis

*For logistic regression, independent variables may be a mixture of continuous and categorical.
**For analysis of covariance, the covariate(s) should preferably be continuous.

5.3 Presenting the scale

Here is the checklist of points to cover when presenting your scale (see Section 1.1):
- statement of what the scale measures
- justification for the scale (uses, advantages over existing measures)
- how the preliminary pool of items was drawn up (details of sources, sampling of sources, any special steps regarding content or face validity)
- description of the sample used for testing
- descriptive statistics (norms): means, standard deviations, ranges (for different samples of subjects, different subscales)
- reliability statistics
- validity statistics
- the scale (instructions, items or examples of items).

5.4 Summary

This chapter described the final steps in presenting the scale, describing how to carry out validity testing. These put the final touches to the basic requirements of developing a scale which measures reliably what it is supposed to measure. The test should be usable by others to obtain results which can be interpreted and compared using the normative data you have produced.

Appendix to Chapter 1

Selecting and presenting tests

A1.1 Examples of test and scale presentation

Three examples have been selected to show the sort of thing that can be assessed in a psychological scale. I have selected slightly novel topics: narcissism, individual responsibility, and quality of cognitive therapy. They show the sort of information that needs to be collected and presented. The examples are summaries of much longer presentations in academic journal articles. You may be able to see where there is room for improvement now and then.

A1.1.1 Narcissistic Personality Inventory (NPI)

The NPI is a relatively modern measure of personality. Part of the development of this measure is described more fully in Raskin & Terry (1988).

Statement of what the scale measures – general narcissism, and seven components: authority, exhibitionism, superiority, vanity, exploitativeness, entitlement and self-sufficiency. Definitions of narcissism are offered from DSM-III (the American Psychiatric Association's *Diagnostic and statistical manual of mental disorders* 1980), Havelock Ellis (1898) and Freud (1914, 1923).

Justification for the scale – the authors offer an extensive survey of the theoretical importance of narcissism, especially in the psychoanalytic and clinical literature. The chief justification appears to be the growing recognition of the clinical importance of narcissistic personality disorder.

How the preliminary pool of items was drawn up – the DSM-III definition describes eight interrelated behaviours. These were used as a starting-point for a pool of 220 dyadic items which were reduced to

54 items in a series of studies using the internal consistency approach (Raskin & Hall 1979). The authors also used Emmons' (1984) principal components analytic work on the NPI as a starting-point for an examination of the distinguishable factors assessed within the NPI.

Description of the sample used for testing – three studies are reported, all using students from the University of California. The first used 1,018 subjects (479 men and 529 women, aged 17–49, mean age 20 years), the second used 57 (28 men and 29 women, mean age 21 years) and the third study used 127 students (65 men and 62 women, aged 17–40, mean age 19 years). Subjects in the second study were paid, and subjects in the third study received academic credit for participation.

Descriptive statistics (norms) – a table gives the inter-correlations between the component subscales and the full scale, for the 40-item NPI. Means, standard deviations and other statistics are reported for the full scale and the seven subscales. The mean of the full scale for the sample of 1,018 students was 15.55 (s.d.=6.66).

Reliability statistics – alphas (coefficient of internal consistency) are quoted as ranging from 0.80 to 0.86 across several studies. The present paper reported a principal components analysis, which produced seven factors listed above, accounting for 49 per cent of the variance, involving pruning the scale to 40 items. Each scale involved at least three marker items with loadings of 0.50 or above.

Validity statistics – a variety of construct validity studies are referred to. The study under description describes two construct validity studies investigating the relationship of full-scale narcissism and the subscales with a variety of measures from observational data, self-report and self-description. Reported significant correlations, according with theory underlying the NPI, range from 0.17 to 0.47.

The scale – The current NPI has 40 paired items. Subjects are asked to mark the member of each pair that they most agree with. For example

A – I have a natural talent for influencing people.
B – I am not good at influencing people
(Authority)
A – I don't care about new fads and fashions
B – I like to start new fads and fashions
(Exhibitionism)
A – My body is nothing special
B – I like to look at my body
(Vanity)

A1.1.2 Individual Responsibility (IR) measure

The IR is a measure of preference for personal responsibility; Franken (1988) describes initial development of the scale.

Statement of what the scale measures – the scale measures individual responsibility: the degree to which the person prefers environments that offer personal initiative, personal freedom and/or personal control.

Justification for the scale – the scale is introduced by suggesting the importance to occupational psychology for identifying preferences and traits that may go along with successful managerial style, as described by Peters & Waterman (1982). IR is suggested as part of a group of preferences and traits, which also includes an active-decisive style (AD) and sensation-seeking. IR is assessed together with AD (but in the description provided in this example, only IR is described).

How the preliminary pool of items was drawn up – paired items were generated to assess whether or not the person prefers to make their own decisions versus having the decisions made by somebody else. These were alternated with items assessing decision-making style (AD).

Description of the sample used for testing – a preliminary pool of items was first tested on a sample of "about 250 students" (numbers of men and women, and age unspecified). This stage of testing was used to select IR and AD items that best differentiated subjects with high AD from those with high IR. The IR measure was then administered to samples of 417 students (176 men and 241 women, mean age 22.6) and 349 non-students (218 males, 131 females, from 12 different occupational groups – all professional and white-collar – with mean ages from 26.6 to 36.9).

Descriptive statistics (norms) – means for the 13 different occupational groups tested ranged from 12.33 to 15.69. Other descriptive statistics include inter-correlations of the IR with the other measures mentioned, within each occupational group.

Reliability and validity statistics – alpha (internal consistency) for the IR scale was 0.48. IR correlated significantly with AD ($r = 0.20$, $p < 0.01$) and with sensation-seeking ($r = 0.24$, $p < 0.01$), but not with Rotter's Internal/External Locus of Control Scale, producing mixed evidence on construct validity. Factor analytic work produced factors that corresponded "reasonably well" with the qualities the scale was designed to measure. The author regards the reliability of the IR scale and its associations with AD and sensation-seeking as modest. Means for different occupational groups suggest some degree of criterion validity: the lowest means are for retail sales and military personnel, and the highest for stockbrokers and lawyers.

The scale – Subjects are asked to select which item from each pair most describes the way they think or feel. For example

A – I prefer to make all my own travel arrangements

B – I prefer "packaged tours"

A – It is the responsibility of the worker to determine how to do the job efficiently

B – It is the job of the manager or supervisor to determine how to do a job efficiently.

Comment – the reliabilities and validities for this scale are not always satisfactory, but sufficient statistics are presented for this to be apparent. Beware of scales which do not present enough statistics.

A1.1.3 Quality of Cognitive Therapy Scale (CTS)

Dobson et al. (1985) describe some of the psychometric properties of the CTS.

Statement of what the scale measures – the scale involves 11 items, assessing aspects of cognitive therapy sessions on agenda; feedback; understanding; interpersonal effectiveness; collaboration; pacing and efficient use of time; empiricism; focus on key cognitions or behaviours; strategy for change; application of cognitive-behavioural techniques; homework.

Justification for the scale – Dobson et al. stress the potential applicability of a reliable measure assessing the quality of therapy (process), and in order to evaluate outcomes.

How the preliminary pool of items was drawn up – the items appear to have been derived from the requirements of cognitive therapy specified by Beck et al. (1979) and Emery et al. (1981), and for psychotherapy in general (Rogers 1957; Truax & Carkhuff 1967; Beck et al. 1979; Arnkoff 1983).

Description of the sample used for testing – 21 psychotherapists (10 psychiatrists and 11 psychologists; 14 men and 7 women) each supplied a one-hour videotape sample of their work. Of these, 12 were tapes of ongoing therapy sessions; 9 were initial consultations. Four raters, all experienced and expert cognitive-behavioural therapists, rated 10 or 11 recorded therapy sessions each, such that each session was rated ("blind") by two raters. In total, 42 sets of ratings were made.

Descriptive statistics (norms) – a drawback of the presentation is that no means (norms) are provided for the CTS.

Reliability statistics – a full range of internal consistency statistics are presented. In spite of the variety of items (and the fact that the scale was proposed to measure two possibly independent dimensions), overall scale alpha = 0.95, suggesting unidimensionality. Only the homework items failed to produce a satisfactory item–total correlation.

Validity statistics – apart from the apparent face and content validity of the items, this presentation does not offer evidence for validity. However, Dobson et al. do present an analysis of variance which shows that between-rater effects were not significant, while between-subject (sessions rated) effects were. This may be regarded (rather loosely) as a form of criterion validity.

The scale – the scale involves Likert-type ratings on the 11 dimensions described at the start of Section A1.1.3.

A1.2 Guidelines on psychological testing

A1.2.1 *Standards for educational and psychological tests*

The American Educational Research Association, American Psychological Association and the National Council on Measurement in Education jointly publish the above-mentioned book; the standards also appear in the Buros Institute's *Mental measurements yearbook*. They are lengthy, and essential for those working professionally with psychological assessment in the USA; they are strongly recommended for those working professionally with psychological assessment in other countries. This brief outline is introductory; the reader is also advised to consult the standards described elsewhere in Appendix 1 and in Appendix 3.

The principal sections of the standards are standards for tests, manuals and reports; standards for reports of research on reliability and validity; and standards for the use of tests. About 300 standards are described, each graded as essential, or very desirable, or desirable. Selected essential standards are summarized below.

Standards for tests, manuals and reports

A1 – A published test should be accompanied by an updated manual or other available information, in which every reasonable effort has been made to follow the recommendations of these standards.

B1 – The test, the manual and all associated material should help users make correct interpretations of the test material, and warn against common misuses.

B2, B3, B4, B5 – The manual should state the recommended purposes and applications of the test, the characteristic(s) measured, the qualifications required for test administration and interpretation, and evidence of reliability and validity and other related research.

C1 – Directions for administration and scoring should enable duplication of the conditions under which norms, reliability and validity were obtained.

D1 – Most tests are interpreted by comparing scores with scores made by other individuals. These are *norm-referenced* tests. Any such tests require the publication of norms in the manual.

D2 – Norms should refer to clearly defined populations.

Standards for reports of research on reliability and validity

E1 – A manual or report should present the evidence of validity for each type of inference for which test use is recommended (and any omissions in this respect should be made clear). Detailed recommendations are given for each type of validity.

F1 – A manual or report should present evidence of reliability, including estimates of the standard error of measurement, so as to enable users to judge whether scores are sufficiently dependable for intended uses of the test (and any omissions in this respect should be made clear). Detailed recommendations are given for each type of reliability.

Standards for the use of tests

G1 – Any test user should have a knowledge of the principles of (psychological) measurement, and of the limitations of test interpretation.

H1 – Choice of tests or other assessments should be based on clearly formulated goals and hypotheses.

I1, I3 – The standardized procedures described in the test manual for administration and accurate scoring.

J1 – A test score should be interpreted as an estimate of performance under specific circumstances, not as an absolute characteristic that will apply in other circumstances.

J5 – In norm-referenced interpretations, scores must be interpreted with reference to appropriate norms. Among many other detailed recommendations, users are warned against bias, and the use of obsolete material.

A1.2.2 *Psychological testing: a guide*

The British Psychological Society Steering Committee on Test Standards publishes the above booklet, which is obtainable from the British Psychological Society, St Andrews House, 48 Princess Road East, Leicester LE1 7DR. The guide points out that tests are used when assessment of one or more psychological attributes are needed, usually in clinical, educational or occupational settings. The booklet is aimed mainly at non-psychologists, and covers an introduction to testing, applications and quality-control issues, advice on what to look for in a test and information on the society's certificates of competence (see Appendix 1.5) and useful publications.

The booklet provides definitions of psychological testing and offers a typology of tests and related measures and their applications. The chief features of quality are reliability, validity and utility, which are defined and discussed. Summary definitions are
- *reliability* – consistency of measurement
- *validity* – relevance of the scores
- *utility* – cost-effectiveness of using the test.

The booklet emphasizes the importance of training in the administration, evaluation and interpretation of tests, pointing out that neglect of these issues can lead to inefficiency and wastage of resources, and injustice and danger to those tested. It offers practical advice on test selection, suggesting that a good test manual should contain the following (the information is summarized as it is generally discussed in some detail in the text of the present book):
- A clear statement of the aims and objectives of the test.
- Brief details of the history of the test's design.
- Information on reliability, usually internal consistency (alphas) or test–retest reliability. Typical figures would be in the range of 0.7–0.95, with adequate numbers in the sample(s) on which the reliabilities are calculated (never less than 30).

- Information on face, content, construct, concurrent and/or predictive validities. The typical range of predictive validities is said to be 0.2–0.45.
- Utility may not be directly mentioned in test manuals, but predictive validity data will be relevant.
- Norms.
- Structure of the test: details of subtests and other aspects of item analysis.
- Bibliography.

A1.2.3 IPM *code on psychological testing*

The code is obtainable from: The Institute of Personnel Management, IPM House, Camp Road, Wimbledon, London SW19 4UX. This booklet covers similar ground to the British Psychological Society's *Psychological testing: a guide*, described above. However,the booklet is geared specifically towards the use of tests in occupational settings: in recruitment and selection; training and development, and counselling.

Therefore in addition to stressing the importance of reliability and validity, the booklet deals with questions important in the occupational setting, such as the following. Is it appropriate to use tests at all? Will they provide additional, relevant information? When used for selection, are the tests relevant to the job and person specification, and chosen on the basis of a job analysis? Are those who will administer, evaluate, interpret and feed back the results competent to do so? Will the tests infringe equality of opportunity (this may happen if different groups of people score differently on the test)?

How will the results be stored and used (test results should be evaluated carefully, in the context of other information about the person)? Have the test norms been updated and verified within the past five years?

The booklet deals with various important legal aspects of test use. Copyright laws prohibit reproduction of test materials (including transferring them into computer versions) without the supplier's permission. Similarly tests may not be adapted or edited without permission; such adaptation produces flawed test results. Test use should not infringe the following legislation:

Data Protection Act 1984

Sex Discrimination Act 1975

Sex Discrimination (NI) Order 1976 as amended
Race Relations Act 1976
Fair Employment Act (NI) as amended
These acts are published by Her Majesty's Stationery Office and may be ordered from HMSO, POB 276, London SW8 5DR, 0171 873 9090. Implications of these acts for employers are contained in the following:
  IPM *code on employee data*
  IPM *equal opportunities code*
  IPM *recruitment code*
which may be ordered from the Institute of Personnel Management (address above).

A1.3 Some publishers of psychological tests

A much more comprehensive list appears in the Buros *Mental measurements yearbook*.

Consulting Psychologists Press Inc., 577 College Avenue, Palo Alto, California 94306, USA.

Educational and Industrial Testing Service (EDITS), San Diego, California 92107, USA.

Hodder & Stoughton, Test Department, Mill Road, Dunton Green, Sevenoaks, Kent TN13 2YA, UK (tel: 01732 450111).

National Foundation for Educational Research, NFER Nelson Publishing Company Ltd, Darville House, 2 Oxford Road East, Windsor, Berks SL4 1DF, UK (tel: 01753 858961 fax: 01753 856830).

Oxford Psychologists Press Ltd, Lambourne House, 311–21 Banbury Road, Oxford OX2 7JH, UK (tel: 01865 510203 fax: 01865 310368).

The Psychological Corporation, Harcourt Brace Jovanovitch, 7500 Old Oak Boulevard, Cleveland, Ohio 44130, USA.

The Psychological Corporation, Harcourt Brace Jovanovitch, Foots Cray High Street, Sidcup, Kent DA14 5HP, UK (tel: 0181 300 3322 fax: 0181 309 0807).

Saville & Holdsworth Ltd, The Old Post House, 81 High Street, Esher, Surrey KT10 9QA, UK (tel: 01372 68634 fax: 01372 62374).

Thames Valley Test Company, 7–9 The Green, Flempton, Bury St Edmunds, Suffolk IP28 6EL, UK (tel: 01284 84608).

A1.4 Measures included in the Mental Health Portfolio

The Mental Health Portfolio is obtainable from National Foundation for Educational Research, NFER Nelson Publishing Company Ltd, Darville House, 2 Oxford Road East, Windsor, Berks SL4 1DF, UK (tel: 01753 858961 fax: 01753 856830). Tests in the portfolio may be photocopied for use by members of the purchasing institution, and the portfolio is an economical alternative to purchase of commercially published tests (especially for those working in institutions which have already purchased the portfolio). However, you may find a suitable published test for which there are no charges for use.

General distress
• General Health Questionnaire

Anxiety
• Fear Questionnaire
• Mobility Inventory for Agoraphobia
• Clinical Anxiety Scale
• Padua Inventory

Stress, coping and social support
• Hassles and Uplifts Scales
• Significant Others Scale
• Coping Responses Inventory

Habit disorder
• Morgan–Russell Assessment Schedule
• Body Shape Questionnaire
• Short Alcohol Dependence Scale

Psychological adjustment to illness
• McGill Pain Questionnaire

Interpersonal difficulties
• Social Activities and Distress Scale
• Inventory of Interpersonal Problems
• Golombok Rust Inventory of Sexual Satisfaction
• Golombok Rust Inventory of Marital State.

A1.5 British Psychological Society's certificates of competence in occupational testing

These certificates are designed for non-psychologists who need to use psychological tests in their professional work. They would normally be redundant for those who hold or expect to gain a psychology degree of a type which would give graduate basis for registration with the British Psychological Society. Further details of these certificates may be obtained from the British Psychological Society, St Andrews House, 48 Princess Road East, Leicester LE1 7DR (tel: 01162 549568). An open learning programme covering level A (Bartram & Lindley 1994) is also available from the British Psychological Society; this package costs £165.

Commercial organizations offering training for these certificates include:

- Team Focus Limited, Hawtrey House, 12 Ray Park Avenue, Maidenhead, Berkshire SL6 8DS (tel: 01628 26264)
- PsyTech International, Icknield House, Eastcheap, Letchworth, Herts SG6 3DA (tel: 01462 482833)

Local university psychology departments may also offer training for these certificates.

These certificates of competence may be issued to psychologists and to non-psychologists. The skills required do not involve test or scale construction; the certificates cover the knowledge and skills required to understand, evaluate, administer, score, interpret, and feedback psychological tests and test results. *Level A* covers the general foundations of testing, and the performance skills associated with test administration and interpretation for group *ability tests*. *Level B* (there will be two level B qualifications) builds on level A competences, covering personality assessment, and the interpretation and use of *personality tests*.

The level A units cover defining assessment needs; basic principles of scaling and standardization; importance of reliability and validity; deciding when psychological tests should or should not be used as part of an assessment process; administering tests to one or more candidates and dealing with scoring procedures; making appropriate use of test results and providing accurate written and oral feedback to clients and candidates; maintaining security and confidentiality of the test materials and the test data.

An intermediate level B certificate is gained by obtaining a level A certificate, and three credits in foundation units, that is, personality theory (1 credit) and personality assessment (2 credits) plus eight credits in test use in both client (employer)-oriented and candidate-oriented assessment contexts, that is, administration (1 credit), interpretation (3 credits) and providing feedback (4 credits).

71

A full level B certificate is gained by obtaining the level A certificate and the intermediate level B credits, plus 15 further credits, comprising a further seven credits in test use and interpretation, using a different instrument, plus eight credits in test choice, that is, approaches to personality assessment and test construction (2 credits), validity and reliability issues (2 credits), computer-based assessment and computer-generated reports (1 credit), and when and how to use personality and interest assessment instruments (3 credits).

A1.6 Some useful tests: an introductory review

The following short survey introduces some (but not all) widely used tests and scales, and mentions some of their advantages and shortcomings. I have generally described tests which I have experience of using. This survey could be useful if you are unfamiliar with the variety of tests and scales available, and have no familiarity with the more commonly used measures. It does not claim to be comprehensive, or even to give a systematic description of the tests covered. The survey is designed to draw your attention to some commonly used tests, and some of their features. Chapter 1 and its appendices offers advice on how to conduct a comprehensive search.

First, it is important to make clear to yourself what you want to assess (it is best to write it down). Think and decide whether the test(s) you are interested in really do assess what you want to assess.

Secondly, most of the tests and scales discussed have user restrictions (see Ch. 1, Section 1.2.3). If you are a student working under qualified supervision, you may be able to use many of them nevertheless, provided no special training is required. Note that it may take some effort to discover whether there are user restrictions. A test published in an academic journal may not necessarily be "public domain", since subsequently the author may have published commercially. Check any stock of published tests you may have access to, check test publishers' catalogues, and if the test does not appear to be published, write to the author for permission to reproduce and to use it. The author's address for correspondence is given in the journal.

Thirdly, who are you testing? The tests and measures discussed below are suitable for use with literate English-speaking adults. If you are working with children, those with disabling conditions, cultural minorities, or any other special groups, you will need to consult with those who have experience in doing assessments of the group(s) concerned.

Finally, if a test sounds likely, check the test handbook or other published description for more details. Do the types of reliability and validity reported meet your needs? For example, if you were looking for a measure that was sensitive to changes as a result of external events, you would probably be more interested in internal consistency and would probably avoid a test with high test–retest reliability (suggesting that it may not readily reflect change).

The rest of this appendix describes various kinds of measures in five groups:

1. Measures of state
2. Measures of trait
3. Measures of social attitudes
4. Measures of social desirability
5. Other measures (by far the largest and most varied group).

For fuller information on each test, consult Buros (who will give supplier details), or the handbook or published journal article describing the test. The tests described have (unless otherwise stated) met at least minimal requirements for reliability and validity as follows:

Reliability – a reported coefficient of at least 0.70 for the scale and for each of any subscales, or adequate factor-analytic derivation.

Validity – adequate and appropriate evidence of at least one of the following forms of validity: concurrent, criterion, predictive, construct, in addition to face and construct validity where these are appropriate.

A1.6.1 Measures of state

A state is transient. A state measure would enable examination of the effect of some happening, whether a natural happening (like a hurricane, or your team winning the cup final) or a research or other intervention. Commonly used measures of state are mainly of emotion, and mainly of negative emotion.

Multiple Affect Adjective Check List
The Multiple Affect Adjective Check List (MAACL: state version; there is also a trait version) (Zuckerman & Lubin 1963) covers three common distress states: depression, anxiety and hostility. It looks formidable, with well over a hundred items, but all that subjects have to do is tick

the words that apply to them, so it can be completed quite rapidly. However, you may have to reassure people that it *does* take only a few moments. It does have some positive mood words on it, which makes it less threatening, but positive mood is not actually assessed: failures to check positive mood words contribute to the negative mood (distress) score. This test has been validated against clinical groups but is not in itself a measure of clinical state. Some words (such as "gay") are ambiguous or culturally loaded. The advantages of the measure are that it assesses hostility as well as the more commonly examined depression and anxiety, it is quick to do (in spite of appearances) and it has been very well researched.

Beck Depression Inventory

Of all negative states, depression is probably the most heavily researched, and of all measures of depression, *The Beck Depression Inventory* (BDI) (Beck & Steer 1987) is probably the most popular. The measure has been well researched, and it does give some idea of *clinical* status. Two main complaints are that some of the questions are rather intrusive (and therefore the measure may be seen as threatening), and it is rather an expensive test. The advantages are relative speed of administration (compared to a "proper" clinical interview and assessment), and lots of published research for you to compare your data with. In view of the expense and the ethical problems, I would avoid this scale unless you really need a measure of clinical state, and you prefer it to the HAD (described below).

Hospital Anxiety and Depression Scale

The Hospital Anxiety and Depression Scale (HAD) (Zigmond & Snaith 1983) has been less widely used than the BDI or the MAACL. It is cheaper than either (you can obtain it in the Mental Health Portfolio: see Appendix 1.4). It also quick, less threatening than the BDI, and the authors have tried to select items to assess depression that are least heavily contaminated by anxiety (and vice versa), and that are unlikely to be contaminated by the presence of physical illness. This is a useful feature since the co-occurrence of depression and anxiety with each other and with physical illness has been a problem for research and assessment of both these very unpleasant conditions. The term "hospital" in the title is a bit misleading; the measure is perfectly appropriate for community and other samples. Although this measure has not been as popular as others, there are 58 references to it on

PsychLit, so there is plenty of published material available for comparison. Validity is reported to be good; the only reliability analysis is of internal consistency, with item–subscale–total correlations ranging from 0.3 to 0.76 (some coefficients are rather low).

State Self-Esteem Scale

The State Self-Esteem Scale (SSES) (Heatherton & Polivy 1991) is relatively recently published, and appears not to have been used much. It seems to meet a need for a measure of state self-esteem in adults, and the authors report satisfactory reliability and validity. The test does not seem to be commercially available, but its publication in a respected research journal suggests that the authors would have no objection to its use at least for research purposes, but it would be advisable to confirm this with the authors.

A1.6.2 Measures of trait

Traits are suggested to be relatively stable and enduring dispositions, so a trait measure ought to have good test–retest reliability in addition to other desirable psychometric properties. Trait measures of personality and of intelligence are most likely to be needed. Only a few of the best known are described here; even among this small selection, use of most is restricted and special training is required.

Eysenck Personality Inventory and Questionnaire

The Eysenck Personality Inventory (EPI) (Eysenck & Eysenck 1964), and the *Eysenck Personality Questionnaire* (EPQ) (Eysenck & Eysenck 1975) were developed by the Eysenck team in London. The main traits assessed are neuroticism (N) and extraversion–introversion (E), but scores on a lie scale (L) (a social desirability measure) and a psychoticism and/or psychopathy (P) score may also be obtained. The measures are quick to administer, and do not need special training; although not free, either test is relatively inexpensive compared to some commercially available tests of personality. These tests do not appear to be threatening or intrusive, though I have some disquiet about some of the P scale items. The tests have good psychometric properties – as indeed they should, since the items were originally selected for their properties in discriminating between clinical and non-clinical groups, and the traits measured were derived by factor analysis. Statistically these tests are sound, and they have some user-friendly features for both testers and testees. They have been widely researched. However, there are some disadvantages. The P measure is not very useful, and it is not very clear what is being measured. The N measure is a mixture of items that appear to gauge depression and anxiety, so one is not getting a pure measure of either. My most serious concern is that the work necessary to establish whether N is truly a measure of trait rather than state has not been done. High scores on N may reflect transient states. However, research using the EPI and related scales has been interpreted as if this was not a possibility. The L scale deserves to be published in its own right. It is a short, fun, user-friendly social desirability measure, much easier to use than any of the social desirability measures which have been published as such.

Minnesota Multiphasic Personality Inventory
The Minnesota Multiphasic Personality Inventory (MMPI) (Hathaway & McKinley 1951, 1967) is possibly the most massively popular of personality tests: there are about 1,500 references in the current *PsychLit* journals database. Psychometric properties are good. The test can be group administered, and is reasonably straightforward to score, though the test is quite a long one. There are 13 scales, assessing (among other things) depression, masculinity–femininity, schizophrenia and social desirability (lie scale).

Myers–Briggs Type Indicator
The distributors suggest that special training is required to administer and score the *Myers–Briggs Type Indicator* (MBTI) (Myers & McCaulley 1985). It has good psychometric properties and is enormously popular, particularly among occupational psychologists, for use in advising people in which types of occupation they may find themselves most comfortable, for example. The test is based on Jung's (1923) theory of personality types, and assesses introversion–extraversion (I and E), sensing-intuition (S and N), thinking–feeling (T and F) and impulse–judgement (P and J). The fact that training is supposed to be needed to administer this test seems over-cautious; the test and its results are very attractive and well liked. Test manuals include profiles of work and relationships styles which are expressed positively, i.e. non-judgementally and non-pejoratively.

Sixteen Personality Factors Questionnaire
Another widely used test is the *16PF (Sixteen Personality Factors Questionnaire)* (Cattell 1965). The test is based on Cattell's important factor-analytic work on personality; it is quite quick and straightforward to administer and to complete. The final result is an interesting personality profile which can be shown to the testee; unfortunately some of the 16 personality factors assessed have rather unintelligible names such premsia, alaxia and praxermia. Unless you use the test a great deal, you may have trouble remembering what they mean and explaining them to testees; more popular terms are on offer, but some of them are a bit uncomplimentary: most people would not be pleased to learn that the test they just kindly did for you revealed them to be "less intelligent", "suspicious", of "low ego-strength" or even "group-tied". It is of interest that one of the factors assessed is intelligence, and this test may be the answer if you want a quick measure of intelligence, in conjunction with some information about personality.

Self-esteem
Coopersmith's (1967) scale was developed for use with children, and adults would find it a bit childish. The best choice for use with adults is probably *Rosenberg*'s (1965) scale, but it is not a perfect choice. Adults sometimes find it rather threatening and intrusive; it is a Guttman-type scale (constructed using methods other than those described in this book, and meeting different reliability criteria). Scoring is described in Burns' (1979) excellent review of self-concept measures as "confusing". There is a longer adult self-concept measure which assesses different aspects of self-esteem (moral, physical, social, etc.): the *Tennessee Self-Concept Scale* (Fitts 1955). This test is rather time-consuming to complete and to score, and expensive to buy.

Intelligence
The measurement of intelligence is a controversial and specialized field. For an estimate of IQ (intelligence quotient) to be made, lengthy sessions of individual testing are normally required, using the *Wechsler Adult Intelligence Scale* (WAIS) (Wechsler 1955), the newer *British Ability Scales* (BAS) (Elliott 1983), or the older *Stanford–Binet* (Terman & Merrill 1960). The constructors of the BAS took into account important theoretical contributions to the understanding of

77

the development of intelligence (notably Piagetian). All these tests are expensive and require special training; they are normally used only for assessments carried out by clinical or educational psychologists. If you have not been introduced to the field, you may not be aware that assessments of cognitive functioning (unlike most assessments of personality, attitudes and values) require quite specialist equipment. Testing involves a fascinating array of props: coloured blocks, stopwatch, mazes, jigsaw puzzles – you need to be quite strong to carry the box of goods to the testing site, and very deft and well practised to record answers, to get out and arrange the next set of equipment for the next test, while checking the details in the test manual, *and* while giving feedback and encouragement to the testee, before the testee gets bored, tense or distracted. (Personality and attitude testing, by contrast, normally requires the testee to read each item and write down their response, or, at most, you (the tester) read out the items and write down the responses.)

Useful, more rapid, group-administered tests of intelligence are available, for example those developed by Alice *Heim* (Heim 1968, 1970; Heim et al. 1983). These tests contain separate measures of verbal, numerical and non-verbal-visual-spatial abilities. When administering these or other group tests, bear in mind that the testee can see how many items there are, and that some look impossible: this does not happen with individually administered tests, where the tester brings out the items one at a time. Testees need to be reassured that the test is designed to be virtually impossible to complete, otherwise they may find the whole experience depressing and frustrating. The *AH5* and *AH6* are for adults of higher ability, and the *AH4* covers the general range of adult ability.

Projective tests
There are a number of projective tests and techniques available. The basic idea of all of them is to present the testee with some "stimulus" – usually a picture, or the beginning of a story – and asking them to describe or complete it. The subject's "responses" are scored for the presence of themes of interest to the tester, and the theory is that people project their wishes or preoccupations into the material that they produce. The most famous of these tests is the *Rorschach* ("inkblot") personality test, in which people are shown a series of patterns which were made by blotting coloured inks on to paper, and asked to describe them. The Rorschach and other projective tests have a

reputation for poor reliability. They generally need special training, in order to achieve scoring that is as reliable as possible. In spite of the massive popularity of the Rorschach, this and other projective tests are probably generally best left to their devotees.

Type A behaviour

Type A behaviour is assessed by a self-report measure, the *Jenkins Activity Survey* (Jenkins et al. 1978, 1979). It assesses the so-called "coronary-prone personality" (competitive, impatient, sense of urgency, drive for success). Although there are scientific disputes surrounding the findings of the team which developed this scale, the measure continues to be popular and is not difficult to use or to score. Conventional reliability statistics (alpha) are suggested to be inappropriate; the item reliabilities presented range from 0.39 to 0.79 (test-retest), and 0.27–0.75 (squared multiple correlation coefficient). The most interesting validity evidence is that high scorers were nearly twice as likely to develop coronary heart disease over a four-year period than were low scorers.

1.6.3 Measures of social attitudes

A wide range of social attitudes and beliefs have been studied. It is worth thinking about whether you are concerned with assessing *attitudes*, which are positively or negatively emotionally toned beliefs, where the investigator is concerned with assessing the positivity or negativity of *feelings* towards the attitude object, or *beliefs*, ideas or cognitions, regarding which the investigator is concerned with the extent to which the person believes them to be *true*.

It is sometimes difficult to decide which is the focus of investigation. The most important group of attitudes and beliefs to be investigated have probably been those to do with conservatism. The assessment of achievement-related motives and beliefs is an interesting chapter in the history of psychology, still of some importance for occupational psychologists, and for personnel and management professionals. More recently, attitudes and beliefs to do with women's roles have attracted some attention, as have those to do with religion, and – of increasing importance for the rapidly expanding field of health psychology – a number of health-related issues, among many others. Three examples are discussed below (others appear in Appendix 1.6.5).

California F

The *California F* (Adorno et al. 1950) is the justly famous traditional measure of *authoritarianism*. The "F" stands for "Potentiality for Fascism". It is one of several scales developed in the late 1940s by a team of social scientists in the USA, refugees from Nazi Germany. The F scale is as much a measure of beliefs and/or personality as it is of attitudes, and it is supposed to assess such traits as concern with power in social relationships, anti-intraception and superstition, and it relates well to "purer" measures of social attitudes assessing anti-semitism, ethnocentrism (belief in the superiority of one's own cultural group) and political and economic conservatism (anti-welfare and anti-equal rights). The F scale has attracted much criticism, including concern about its applicability to the study of left-wing authoritarianism, and concern about the fact that none of the items is negatively worded (reverse-meaning). The scale is hardly a contemporary one and it seems surprising that most of the items still sound relevant and intelligible.

Wilson–Patterson C

The *Wilson–Patterson C (Conservatism)* (Wilson & Patterson 1968) is a more modern measure of conservatism in social attitudes and beliefs than the California F. Some of the items may be found puzzling or dated by the tester or by testees, such as fluoridation, pyjama parties, birching and learning Latin. It has good psychometric properties, it is easy to administer and to score, and in spite of the momentary bewilderment that may be caused by some items, people appear to enjoy completing this scale, which is quick and quite interesting. Psychometric properties are good. Even the bewildering items cause amusement and interest, rather than the anger or fear which may be provoked by some items on some scales.

Burns Life Styles for Women

The *Burns Life Styles for Women* (Burns 1974) assesses the extent to which the person feels that it is appropriate for women to pursue a career regardless of other commitments, or whether women should prioritize marriage, homemaking and child-care. It was developed at a time when "feminism" was a hot topic of debate, and it still taps concerns that are important to many women, especially the more highly educated. The scale would not be appropriate for use in less privileged groups. The scale is not really appropriate for use on men either, although the author suggests that it can be administered to men by asking them to say how their ideal woman should think. The men tested by Burns certainly had a more "traditional" view of women's life styles than did the women, but this may have been because of the way men were asked to complete the scale. It is quick to do, easy to administer (when testing those for whom it is appropriate, i.e. middle-class women), easy to score, quite interesting, and not apparently too threatening. Reliability is good.

1.6.4 Measures of social desirability

This small group of tests was developed to address a very interesting concern of psychometricians. There are a number of ways in which answers to tests, scales and other psychological measures may be affected by so-called "response biases". One response bias goes by the grand name of "acquiescence response set", and also the more intelligible name "yea-saying". It was briefly discussed in Chapter 2, where it was advised that it was often useful to write some items that were negatively worded (reverse-meaning), to deal with any tendency that people may have to agree with anything, especially if it comes from an official-looking source. Chapter 2 also discussed social desirability, the tendency to give answers or to endorse responses which appear to be socially desirable, correct, or "good" in some other way, but which may not be the best reflection of the person's feelings or beliefs. Attempts have been made to assess social desirability, and although they are somewhat culture-bound, there are occasions when one of the following measures (or another social desirability measure) may be useful.

Lie scales
The *short L (lie) scale of the* EPI (see above) is incorporated in the Eysenck Personality Inventory; although it is a good measure of social desirability, it may not be worthwhile unless you want to assess neuroticism or introversion–extraversion (also assessed in the EPI). The *Minnesota Multiphasic Personality Inventory* (MMPI) also incorporates a *Lie scale*; the MMPI is a massive test and clearly it is even less worth administering the whole test for the sake of the Lie scale score.

Social desirability scales
The *Marlowe–Crowne* SDS *(Social Desirability Scale)* (Crowne & Marlowe 1960) was developed to avoid the problem that responses to social desirability items may be contaminated by psychopathology. The scale has good psychometric properties, and was shown to be less strongly related to several measures of psychopathology than the *Edwards* SDS *(Social Desirability Scale)* (Edwards 1957). Although it looks lengthy (and therefore daunting) it does not take long to do because people just have to tick those items that are generally applicable to them, and the items come over as interesting and thought-provoking (e.g. "I have never intensely disliked anyone") rather than threatening.

A1.6.5 Other measures

A tremendous gamut of psychological constructs, not covered under any of the above headings, can be assessed. Here is very small sample.

Stress
In popular parlance, stress is a state, but among psychologists, the term stress is generally used to describe a set of conditions which involves a change to customary modes of behaviour, and which a person *may* not have the resources to cope with. An early and popular stress measurement scale was the *Holmes–Rahe Social Readjustment Scale* (Holmes & Rahe 1967). This lists a number of types of life-event (such as birthdays, violations of the law, trouble with in-laws) and people are asked to indicate which have happened to them or to those close to them in the previous year (or in whatever period is appropriate). Each event has a weighting, an agreed index of the "average" severity of that event, and a person's score is the total of the weightings of those events they have experienced. The main problem with the Holmes–Rahe scale is that one has no idea of how any event actually impacted on the person in practice (trouble with in-laws could range from a disabling assault, to a mild disagreement about the colour scheme for new carpets, which was eventually resolved), and thus how much their life was disrupted. Another problem with the Holmes–Rahe is that considerable research effort showed poor predictive validity. A better modern alternative might be the *Hassles and Uplifts Scale* (which can be administered as two separate scales)

(Kanner et al. 1981; available in the Mental Health Portfolio – see Appendix 1.4). This measure has been claimed to be better at predicting distress and illness outcomes than the Holmes–Rahe, but testees may get irritated and resentful because of its length and repetitiousness, even if only the Hassles part is used (both scales together have over 250 items). So-called context-sensitive stress measures (the original one is the *Life Events and Difficulties Schedule*: G. W. Brown & Harris 1978) are probably the best predictors of distress and illness outcomes, and they are liked by interviewees. However, they are extremely labour-intensive, typically needing an interview of well over an hour and sometimes several hours, and require lengthy training both in interviewing and coding, and are therefore not advised for run-of-the-mill use.

Religion
A number of aspects of religious belief, experience and feeling have been assessed. Reported reliabilities are sometimes a bit low. There are three useful measures, in terms of their relations to other factors. The *Religious Life Inventory* (Batson et al. 1993) assesses extrinsic, intrinsic and quest religious orientation; this scale is based on Batson's (1976) factor-analytic work using items developed by earlier workers. *Spiritual support* (Maton 1989) is suggested to be a stress-buffering factor. The scale is brief, but has a very high reported reliability, and the validity work is impressive. Hood's (1975) *Religious experience* has several subscales, which survived factor-analysis satisfactorily. Construct validity is satisfactory. The scale measures reported mystical-type experiences.

Religious affiliation, religious practice and attendance and other religious factors should be assessed in questionnaire measures developed to suit the groups investigated. It is normally very difficult to use religion measures on groups other than those for which they were developed: for example Muslims, Jews and other non-Christians are disconcerted or irritated when asked about church attendance, or even "attendance" at "place of worship" (in some religions, "worship" especially by women is done mainly at home). Professing agnostics are another group that need special attention when assessing religion. You will therefore probably have to develop your own set of questions, or use a questionnaire developed by someone else who has worked on the same group.

Values

The *Allport–Vernon Study of Values* (Allport & Vernon 1960) uses a forced-choice format and assesses people on self-reported interest in several general areas of activity (social, religious, political, etc.). *Rokeach's* (1969) checklist involves more specific values (such as salvation, forgiving) grouped under two general headings (means, or instrumental, and ends, or terminal). Both measures seem to be non-threatening and quite thought-provoking. The forced-choice format of the Allport–Vernon does not reveal if a person has a generally high (or generally low) interest in all the areas examined; the measure just reveals *comparative* levels of self-reported interest in different areas, for example whether the person regards "Art" as more important than, say, their social life. Some subjects may find it annoying to have to be forced to choose between two equally desirable or undesirable alternatives; this is a problem with the forced-choice format whenever it is used to assess opinions, values or other non-factual constructs.

Social support

Social support is an important area of current investigation. The *Quality of Relationships Inventory* (QRI) (Pierce et al. 1991) and the *Significant Others Scale* (SOS) (Power et al. 1988) are both usable measures, with good psychometric properties. The QRI is available on application to the authors, while the SOS is available in the Mental Health Portfolio. The QRI uses a Likert format, and assesses support (emotional), conflict and depth in a given relationship. The SOS assesses emotional and practical support, both perceived and ideal, in a given relationship, and has the advantage of a brief form (four items) as well as a longer form.

Locus of control

Locus of control or causal expectancy is the extent to which the person feels that events are caused by internal or external factors. *Rotter's* (1966) and *Levinson's* (1973) generalized scales are both still useful measures of generalized locus of control. Levinson's measure is probably more useful in that it distinguishes between two types of external locus of control: luck and chance on the one hand, and powerful others. Some investigators, however, prefer to use measures which are specific to the area of behaviour under investigation.

Health
Many measures have been developed in the rapidly expanding area of health psychology, including the classic *McGill Pain Questionnaire* (MPQ) (Melzack 1975) assessing quality and intensity of pain, measures of *health beliefs* (e.g. Given et al. 1983; Bradley et al. 1987) and *condition-specific measures of locus of control* (e.g. Bradley et al. 1987). The MPQ is available in the Mental Health Portfolio.

Need achievement
In the classical research, achievement-related motives and needs (need for achievement, fear of failure, fear of success) were assessed by projective tests, which often have reliability problems, and which require training. Attempts have been made to develop scales assessing need achievement, for example Smith (1973). My experience of using Smith's scale has been that it is easy to deal with, but unfortunately does not give very good discrimination between testees in groups of students (students get a moderately high score). It may give a wider range of scores in the general population; indeed Smith reported a significant difference in scores between volunteer testees and men listed in *Who's who*. Smith's reliability analysis shows only item–total correlations – quite low ones – and a rather unimpressive split-half reliability of 0.56. The literature on need achievement has reflected only low associations between need achievement and actual achievement in men, and no consistent associations for women at all. It is therefore unlikely that anyone would be considering assessing need achievement for assessment purposes when there is no measure with good predictive validity. For research – and assessment – purposes, it would be preferable to develop an achievement-need scale specific to the domain of achievement you are interested in. Smith's test could be useful in circumstances where a quick and friendly measure of general need-achievement is needed, provided the success or failure of your study does not hinge solely on this test.

Psychotherapy
There has been a development of attempts to monitor and measure the quality of therapy, and to assess outcome. Outcome measures will depend to an extent on the type of therapy, as therapeutic interventions are on different levels and many effects would be specific to some types of therapy only. Those investigating therapeutic outcome, however, will probably want to include perhaps one measure of

"minor" psychiatric morbidity, distress, or personality (such as the MAACL, HAD, EPI or EPQ, 16PF). *Dobson* et al.'s (1985) measure (described in Section A1.1.3) was developed by using observer ratings, but this and similar measures could be used both by clients and therapists.

Appendix to Chapter 3

Ethical guidelines for testing

There are a number of academic and professional organizations offering ethical guidelines for testing and research. The essential points of ethics appear in Chapters 1, 2 and 3. The following appendices offer further details of some of these professional guidelines, as follows:

1. The American Psychological Association's (1985) *Standards for educational and psychological tests* are very lengthy, being published in book form. They also appear in the Buros *Mental measurements yearbook*. A summary of the main features was given in Appendix 1.2.1.

2. The Australian Psychological Society's (1994) *Code of professional conduct* offers concise guidelines for administering, scoring and interpreting tests. Extracts appear in Appendices 3.1, 3.2 and 3.3.

3. The Royal Holloway University of London's (1988) *Ethical Committee notes for guidance* give a concise statement of the minimal requirements for good practice in research involving human subjects. It is quoted in Appendix 3.4.

4. The Medical Research Council (1992) offers a useful booklet of guidelines for research using medical procedures or patients (see Appendix 3.5).

A3.1 Australian Psychological Society's *Code of professional conduct*

The code may be obtained from the Australian Psychological Society, POB 126, Carlton South 3053, Victoria, Australia. This code is the most recent at the time of writing, and includes a detailed supplement on the use of psychological tests, drawing on the codes of both the American Psychological Association and the British Psychological

Society as well as other sources. The guidelines are geared towards the needs of users employing psychological tests for assessment and guidance rather than research, but many of the provisions are important in research as well as assessment.

This appendix covers some general relevant features of the code, and Appendices 3.2 and 3.3 cover more specific features. The code covers the professional conduct of psychologists in the following areas: general principles of conduct including responsibility, competence and propriety; assessment procedures; consulting relationships; teaching of psychology; supervision and training; research; public statements; and professional relationships. The code offers more detailed guidelines in specific areas, including client/psychologist physical contact, and psychological test interpretation and report writing.

The most relevant of the above guidelines are on *assessment procedures*. The code of practice here includes the necessity for:

- appropriate assessments that are administered and interpreted accurately
- ensuring that assessments are reliable, valid and not obsolete
- confidentiality
- ensuring that assessments are by appropriately trained and qualified people.

It is unlikely that your testing procedure will call for *physical contact*. This should be avoided, as should any other verbal or non-verbal behaviour which might be construed as sexual or invasive.

A3.2 Conducting an individual testing session

In a supplement (Kendall et al. 1994) to the Australian Psychological Society's *Code of professional conduct*, it is suggested that those conducting testing sessions should

- establish rapport, to minimize anxiety and maximize motivation
- practise test administration before doing "real" testing
- adhere strictly to instructions for administration, and to verbatim instructions
- watch for signs of stress, boredom, anxiety or fatigue
- provide encouragement without revealing correctness or incorrectness, approval or disapproval of responses (unless this is called for as part of test administration).

A3.3 Feedback

These suggestions for good practice with regard to the giving of feedback are based on Kendall et al. (1994), who provide a much fuller set of guidelines. When introducing the session, state that feedback will (or could) be given (if desired). State that tests of personality, attitude, mood and the like depend on *self-report*, and therefore the results depend on how the person has chosen to respond. If and when results are given, they should be given as fully as possible, and without the use of evaluative and possibly damaging terms (e.g. "failure", "better", "worse"). Feedback which may be damaging or offensive should not be given.

A3.4 Royal Holloway University of London's *Ethical committee notes for guidance*

The essentials of these guidelines were mentioned in Chapters 1, 2 and 3. They are quoted more fully here.

1. The following are general principles to be followed by all investigators who carry out investigations involving human subjects:
    (a) subjects should be told as much as possible about the investigation that they are being asked to take part in, and their explicit consent must be obtained;
    (b) where deception is involved in any investigation, subjects should be carefully debriefed, and the right of subjects to withhold the data collected about them in such an investigation should be respected;
    (c) the data obtained about a subject should be kept strictly confidential (and, if held on a computer, the use of those data should conform with the requirements of the Data Protection Act);
    (d) the data collected in an investigation should not be used for purposes different from those originally specified without the subject's consent;
    (e) it should be made clear to a subject that he or she may withdraw from the investigation at any time without giving a reason.
2. The approval of the ethical committee must be obtained in advance for any investigations involving human subjects which might give rise to ethical problems. Section 3 below gives a guide

to the kinds of investigations for which approval would normally be required.

3. It is not possible to specify in advance precisely what constitutes an investigation which might give rise to ethical problems. However, the committee would normally wish to see the details of proposed investigations which involve any of the following:

   (a) the administration of drugs (including alcohol and caffeine);

   (b) the use of invasive procedures (e.g. the taking of samples or the introduction of electrodes);

   (c) doubt about the subject's capacity to give consent to take part in the investigation (for example, in studies of young children, or the mentally handicapped);

   (d) the subject is suffering, or potentially suffering distress or anxiety or physical discomfort;

   (e) deception – with regard to what will happen during the investigation, to the real purpose of the investigation, or to the basis on which the subjects are selected;

   (f) patients as subjects;

   (g) asking subjects sensitive questions which encroach on their privacy to a degree which might be considered by the subjects as offensive or stressful to answer (e.g. questions about sexual preferences or political convictions).

A3.5 Medical Research Council's guidelines for medical research

A set of guidelines for medical investigators is the Medical Research Council's *Responsibility in investigations on human participants and material on personal information* (1992), which is obtainable from the Medical Research Council, 20 Park Crescent, London W1N 4AL. These guidelines should be consulted if you are doing a study involving any kind of medical intervention, and/or if you are using patients.

Appendix to Chapter 4
Reliability and related statistics

Notes on statistics packages

The specific instructions for computing in the appendices are for SPSS and CSS users. Full instructions are given for carrying out the necessary statistical tests for the main types of reliability, using SPSS-PC (and SPSS-X). Briefer instructions are given for SPSS for Windows and for CSS, and if you are using these, you may occasionally find helpful the fuller explanations given along with SPSS-PC, especially in understanding the output. Some suggestions are made for those with statistics software that has no reliability facility, and for those without a computer.

SPSS exists in three main versions: SPSS-PC, SPSS-X and SPSS for Windows. Commands are given for SPSS-PC and these are usually identical for SPSS-X. SPSS for Windows involves very different procedures and these have been specified separately. West (1991) and Foster (1993) provide fuller guides to the general use of SPSS, particularly by psychologists. West covers SPSS-PC and SPSS-X (but not Windows), while Foster covers SPSS-PC and SPSS for Windows (but not SPSS-X). Unfortunately, neither covers reliability (if they did, there would be less need for this book), and neither book covers CSS.

CSS/Statistica is a user-friendly set of packages, available in IBM and Macintosh versions. Note that a statistics package called SAS also contains a reliability facility. However, it has not been possible to include instructions for SAS in this book.

The UK addresses of the suppliers are as follows. For SPSS: SPSS UK Ltd, SPSS House, 5 London Street, Chertsey, Surrey KT16 8AP. For CSS/Statistica: Statsoft UK Ltd, Icknield House, Eastcheap, Letchworth, Herts SG6 3DA.

A4.1 Types of data, coding and statistics

You need to be aware what kind of number-scale you are using when you code your data. The type of number-scale will affect the choice of statistics that are appropriate. Consult the guide below (and, if necessary, Section 5.2.6) or a suitable book (e.g. Coolican 1990; de Vaus 1993) or an appropriate person if you feel unsure on any of the points.

Interval data

Age and other numerical data (such as number of children, years of education and the like) can be entered straight on to the computer. It is called interval data because you know the size of the interval between two numbers – the difference between 3 and 2 is the same as the difference between 2 and 1. If this sounds like a strange thing to be concerned about, be assured that it *is* important. It is quite likely that some of the data you deal with will not be interval data: other types of data are described below, and in Table A4.1. Interval data are suitable for *parametric* statistical analysis, including anova, Pearson correlation, t-test and multiple regression analysis.

Ordered (or ordinal) data

Here the data may look like numerical data, but there is a difference. With ordinal data you can be sure only that one number is greater than another, but you cannot be sure by how much. If a subject ranks three brands of chocolate in order of preference, such that brand X comes first (rank = 1), brand Y comes second (rank = 2) and brand Z comes third (rank = 3), then we know that 1, 2 and 3 are in order of magnitude, but we do not know anything about the size of the intervals between them; the subject might like brand X far better than brand Y, while brand Y is only a bit nicer than brand Z. Ordinal data may be used in *non-parametric* statistics, suitable for ordinal data, such as Mann–Whitney U, Kendall's tau and Jonkheere's Trend Test. In some cases it may be useful to treat the data as categorical (see below), but never treat them as interval data. Taking the most likely scenarios, you can use ordinal data in cross-tabs and chi-squares, but not in an anova.

Nominal (or categorical) data

Here you do not even know that one number is greater or less than another number. Numbers are just used to indicate category *differences*. In Table A4.1 there are three categories for food taste: sweet,

Table A4.1 Different types of number scales: interval, ordinal and nominal.

Type of scale	Type of snack	Interval Rating for nutrition (1-7)	Ordinal Order of preference	Nominal Taste (sweet = 1, spicy = 2 bland = 3)
Data from	Chocolate	7	5	1
one subject	Pizza	4	3	2
	Crisps	4	4	2
	Nuts	1	1	3
	Muesli-bar	2	2	1
Descriptive statistics	–	Range, means standard deviations	(Range)	Frequencies, cross-tabs
Inferential statistics		Parametric: e.g. anova, t-test, Pearson correlation, multiple regression	Non-parametric for ordinal data, e.g. Kruskal–Wallis anova, Spearman correlation	Non-parametric for nominal data, e.g. chi-square, loglinear analysis

spicy and bland. If you are going to code these, you should represent them by numbers (because computer statistical packages do not like and cannot normally use alphabetical data). The numbers 1, 2 and 3 are not ordered. It can be very advantageous to have just two categories (rather than more than two); this is called *dichotomous* data. Statistics and interpretation become much clearer and simpler, and important statistics are possible with dichotomous data. Notably, statistics packages can run correlations and reliability statistics on dichotomous data (the techniques are called, respectively, point biserial correlation and the Kuder–Richardson KR–20 reliability coefficient). Unlike categorical data with more than two categories, dichotomous data are ordered. The moral of all this is to try and reduce categorical data to dichotomies, where it is sensible to do so. You do not have to do this when you code the data; you can make many categories and then collapse them into two when you are computing, using a temporary or permanent recode.

Rating scales
Are the ratings interval or ordinal scales? If subjects rate their liking for chocolate on a 5-point scale, and brand X gets a 5, brand Y gets a 4

and brand Z gets a 3, is the difference between the 5 and the 4 the same as the difference between the 4 and the 3. Generally, rating scales may be treated as interval scales, unless you suspect the contrary. Likert (1932) suggested, when he developed his method of scale construction involving rating, that the intervals in such rating scales should be *equal-appearing*.

Table A4.2 Sample questionnaire.

Questionnaire on prayer

We are studying people's views on the uses of prayer.
Your answers to the following questions would be very helpful. Your answers will be confidential and anonymous, identified only by a code number. You need not answer any questions that you would prefer to leave unanswered.

Thank you

Date_____(do not code)
Your age_____(enter as given)
Male/female_____(1 = male, 0 = female)
Current marital status (circle one): (code 1 if currently in stable relationship; i.e. married, engaged or cohabiting, 0 otherwise)
  married (1)   engaged (1)   single (0)   cohabiting (1)   divorced (0)
  widowed (0)   separated (0)
Number of children, if any_____(enter as given)
Their ages_____(code 1 if any under 18, 0 otherwise)
Your occupation_____(code 1 if earning, 0 otherwise)
If married, your spouse's occupation_____
  (code 1 if earning, 0 otherwise)
Do you belong to any church, mosque or synagogue?_____
  (Yes = 1, No= 0)
If yes, which?_____
  (Strong ritual demands = 1, Lower ritual demands = 0)
How often do you attend?(circle one)
  daily   weekly   monthly   occasionally   never
  (daily = 4, weekly = 3, monthly = 2, occasionally = 1, never = 0)
How often do you pray? (circle one)
  daily   weekly   monthly   occasionally   never
  (daily = 4, weekly = 3, monthly = 2, occasionally = 1, never = 0)
How often do you study religious texts? (circle one)
  daily   weekly   monthly   occasionally   never
  (daily = 4, weekly = 3, monthly = 2, occasionally = 1, never = 0)

Table A4.3 Sample coding.

ID_1_____

Your age_22_____

Male/female_male_____ 1

Current marital status (circle one):
married   engaged   <u>single</u>   cohabiting   divorced
widowed   separated   0

Number of children, if any_0_____

Their ages_–_____ 0

Your occupation_student_____ 0

If married, your spouse's occupation_–_____ 99

Do you belong to any church, mosque or synagogue?_no_____

If yes, which?_–_____ 99

How often do you attend?(circle one)
daily   weekly   monthly   <u>occasionally</u>   never   1

How often do you pray? (circle one)
daily   weekly   monthly   occasionally   <u>never</u>   0

How often do you study religious texts? (circle one)
daily   weekly   monthly   <u>occasionally</u>   never   1

A4.2 Example of coding

Table A4.2 gives a simple coding scheme for the beginning of the questionnaire shown in Chapter 2; many others could have been devised. The answers to the "test" part of the questionnaire (the questions on prayer, in the example) do not need any special coding. They can be entered on to the computer database just as they were given. Most of the answers to the first part of the questionnaire, which deals with background, socio-demographic information need to be coded before they can be entered on to the computer. There are coding schemes in which some variables like marital status, details of children, occupation and religious membership have been reduced to simple 0/1 dichotomies, to make statistics more straightforward, but you may wish to use a more elaborate categorization and reduce it later.

Table A4.3 shows the answers, and their coded versions, of a hypothetical subject on this first part of the questionnaire.

A4.3 Making a database

This supplement is for computer illiterates. It will enable you to get going. Do not let it prevent you from using a better method if you have one.

A4.3.1 Starting the database

Here is how to get into some of the programs in which you can make a database:

In Word Perfect
When you turn on the computer and the prompt appears, get into Word Perfect by typing:

> wp

(Do not type the prompt sign >: you can put in commands only in response to this prompt sign.) Follow this by pressing the "enter" key, which is often just marked with a bent arrow. You can then enter your data by typing them in. Start a new line for each subject, and leave a space between each piece of data. Save the data file by pressing F10, and following the menu instructions. When necessary, the database can be turned into an ASCII (DOS) file by pressing Ctrl+F5 and following instructions to create a DOS file, as follows:
Press Ctrl+F5 (simultaneously)
Press (select) 1 (DOS text)
Press (select) 1 (Save)
Name the DOS file (not an identical name to your data file); use e.g. a:prayer.dos
Press "Enter"

In DOS
A modern version of DOS (5.0 or later) has good facilities for making databases (older ones do not), and function quite well as simple word-processors. When the C prompt appears, type

> edit

Follow this by pressing the "enter" key. Now press the "esc" key; this should clear the screen, and you can start entering data. When you want to save data, the first time you do this is as follows:

Press "alt"

Select "file" (make sure the cursor is on the "file" option at the top of the screen, and press "enter")

Either select "save" on the screen using the cursor, and then press "enter"

Or, type S, name the file (e.g. type a:prayer.dat) and press "enter"

You can carry on entering data now, or *exit* by

Press "alt"

Select "file"

Select "exit" or type X

If you continue entering data, you can save your new entries in the same file as before by

Press "alt"

Select "file"

Select "save" or type S

For example, if the hypothetical subject gets the ID number 1, the data are going to look like this:

1 22 1 0 0 0 0 99 0 99 1 0 1 2 5 3 4 3 3 2 4

I have entered answers to the "prayer" items 1 to 8 just as they stand, because the computer can recode the negatively worded ones. In the examples that use this database, I shall just use the eight prayer items on the questionnaire as shown. In reality, there are usually many more.

To add more data at a later time

> edit filename (e.g. a:prayer.dat)

This should get your database back, ready for you to start work on.

Using DOS for data entry has the advantage that the database can be processed by (almost) any statistics package. A database can be made in SPSS-PC but it is a bit awkward. It is easier to use DOS, word-processor or spreadsheet.

In SPSS for Windows

Click on title bar of Data Editor Window

Ctrl + Home (if necessary: the highlight should be in the top left-hand cell)

Type in the data. Each piece of data should appear in a box in the spreadsheet. Press "enter" (bent arrow key) to put each piece of data in the highlighted cell. It is usually easiest to type in the data moving horizontally across the spreadsheet. Enter the subject's ID number in the left-hand cell of each horizontal line, and then use the right-arrow key to move to each new cell. Move to a new line for each new case. For missing data, just leave the relevant cell(s) empty. When correcting data, move the highlight to the cell needing correction, type in the correct entry, and press "enter".

To copy or move sections of data: use click/drag to highlight the section to be moved.

Select Edit, and click on Copy or Cut (as appropriate)

Move the cursor to the cell where the section is to be pasted, and click

Select Edit/Paste.

To name variables: when you have entered your data (or before you have finished, if you wish), enter names for variables. Each column contains data for each variable: move the highlight to *any* cell in the column, select Data/Define variable, click, type the variable name in the dialogue box which appears, and press "enter". If you wish, you can use the *Change Settings* area in the dialogue box to define the variable: give a full description of the variable, and the value labels. For example: married = whether now-married or not. Now-married = 1, not-now-married = 0.

To recode any reverse-meaning items:

Select Recode/Into Same Variables

Enter variables to be recoded by entering them into the Variables list

Select the Old and New Values button

Enter the old value in the Old Values box (e.g. 5)

Enter the new value in the New Values box (e.g. 1)

Click on the Add button.

To save data: check that the Data Editor is in the active window (dark or coloured title bar).

Select File/Save As. A Save As Data File dialogue box will appear

Type in the filename (e.g. religion.sav).

If you want to save on a floppy disc, click on [-A-] in the field headed Directories. In the bottom of the dialogue box, select SPSS and click (this saves the data in SPSS for Windows format; if for any reason you wish to select another format, do so). Select OK and click. Note that it is advisable to use the filename extension .SAV when naming and saving data files in SPSS for Windows.

To retrieve data: select File/Open Data. A dialogue box will appear. Either type in filename (e.g. a:prayer.sav). Or double-click on [-A-] in the Directories box. All files on your floppy disc ending in .SAV will be listed. Select the file to be retrieved and click. Check that the filename in the Name box is indeed the file you want, select OK and click. The data file may now be edited (or analyzed).

In CSS

Select D (data management) from the opening Main Menu, using the highlight (cursor), and press "enter". The menu that appears should be headed "Data Management". Move the highlight to C (Create new data file) and press "enter" (bent arrow key). Type in a name for your file (e.g. prayer.dat) and press "enter". Next type in the number of variables (e.g. 21) and press "enter". Then type in the number of cases (the number of people who did your questionnaire or test) (e.g. 50) and press "enter".

The next piece of information asked for is about the display format: how many digits to allow for before and after the decimal place. It is usually all right to accept the default format, so you can just press "enter" at this point. However, you may find the default option (which prints four digits before the decimal point and two digits after: dddd.dd) a bit irritating, especially if you have a lot of variables with only one digit, so you could change the display format to dd for one-digit variables (CSS won't normally accept d as a format); dd.dd is a useful format for most other purposes. If your entry has more digits after the decimal point, CSS will just round-up or round-down.

The next piece of information is about the number to be assigned to missing values, and it is usually all right to accept the default value, so just press "enter" at this point.

A new menu headed "Variable Specifications" should appear. Use the arrow cursor keys to move around this menu and to enter variable names. Thus, move the highlight to the top of the column headed "Var name", and type in the name of the first variable (e.g. ID), and press "enter". Enter the variable names in the "Var name" column, pressing "enter" each time. You can usually accept the default options for format and missing values, but they can be altered if desired; for example, the format could be altered to "dd" for 1-digit variables. When you have finished, press "enter", and then "Y". A spreadsheet should appear.

Type in the data. Each piece of data should appear in a cell in the spreadsheet. Press "enter" to put each piece of data in the highlighted position. It is usually easiest to type in the data moving horizontally across the spreadsheet. Enter the subject's ID number in the left-hand cell of each horizontal line, and then use the right-arrow key to move to each new cell. Move to a new line for each new case.

Missing data: just leave the relevant cell(s) empty, or type "M". (CSS has a value for missing values which it will enter automatically, but this will not appear on the screen. If you wish to change the number used for missing values, press "R" to use the variable specifications menu; if in doubt, consult the CSS handbook.)

Correcting data: move the highlight to the cell needing correction, press the Space Bar to display the number to be edited at the top of the screen. Use the arrow and delete keys to delete. Enter the desired number and press the "enter" key.

Recode any reverse meaning items.

Save data: press "esc", enter "D", and accept (or enter if you have not done so yet) the filename and header. Press "enter".

To retrieve data for further additions and changes: if you wish to alter your data *without* adding new variables, select E (edit/update current data) from the main (Data Management) menu screen. Press Shift+F1, type in the name of the data file and press "enter". Press E to start editing. The data can be modified using the cursor keys to more around the database, and the "Delete" key as appropriate.

If you want to *add new variables*, select V (edit/update variable specifications) from the main (Data Management) menu. Type in the name of the data file and press "enter". Add the new variable name(s) in the Variable Specifications screen. When you have finished, press "enter" and type Y.

A4.3.2 Checking a database with SPSS-PC (-X)

This involves manoeuvring in and out of SPSS. (This type of check is not necessary if you have used a spreadsheet for data entry, because you should have entered the correct number of pieces of data.)

Get the SPSS prompt onto the screen. On a PC this would be done by:

Either type spss
Or type spsspc
Or type cd spss
Followed by spsspc

This will get you the SPSS scratchpad and menus. It is easier to get rid of these (although the menus can be helpful on some occasions). Do this as follows:

Press F10

Move cursor to "exit to prompt"

Press "enter"

The SPSS/PC> prompt will appear on the screen. Now you can summon your database, and check that you have the correct number of pieces of data for each subject (assume the data are on a floppy disc in the a: drive, and note that the sign > indicates the presence of the prompt – it is not part of the command you have to put in):

> data list file = 'a:prayer.dat' free/id age sex married kids earn spousearn relig attend pray text prayer1 to prayer8.

> list var = id.

If you have the correct number of pieces of data for each subject, then the ID numbers should appear on the screen in order. If you have made a mistake, then you will get one or more ID numbers in order, then a messy string of bits of data. For example

1

2

3

4

0

9.7

34

2

3.01

etc.

If there is an error in the number of pieces of data entered, the last ID number to appear in order is the number of the subject for whom you entered too few or too many pieces of data. In the above example, it was the person with ID number 4. Note this number, and then leave SPSS in order to tidy up your original data file. The command in SPSS-PC is

> stop

Call up your original database and correct the problem. Then go back to SPSS and try again from

>data list file etc.

until

> list var = id.

produces a string of ID numbers in the correct order.

You should then look over your database for other errors. The command

> list.

will produce all your data on the screen without having to go back to the original database. If you have to interrupt this (it can get very time-consuming), press

Ctrl+C

at the same time, and you will get back to the prompt.

It is easier to check a large database on paper than on the screen; to get a print out you could leave SPSS (use the stop command). When the prompt appears on the screen, type

> print filename (e.g. a:prayer dat)

A4.3.3 Making a system file in SPSS-PC (-X)

At this point, you could decide whether you want to make an SPSS system file. This is worth doing if you are using SPSS-PC or SPSS-X, and are likely to keep coming back to do statistics on the data. It saves you having to repeat the data list file command with all the variable names, plus information about missing values, whenever you want to do more analyses on your data.

To make a system file you repeat the command beginning

> data list file . . .

Now enter information about missing values. If you used the same value (say, 99) for each variable, then the command would be:

>missing values age to prayer8 (99).

Recode any negatively worded (reverse-meaning) items:

>recode prayer2 prayer4 prayer6 prayer8 (5 = 1) (4 = 2) (2 = 4) (1 = 5).

You need not compute preliminary total scores for each subject at all if you are working in SPSS, since SPSS will do this for you in the reliability statistics, and you may never need to know them. If you want to compute the preliminary totals at this point, you can use the compute command, as follows:

>compute total = prayer1+prayer2+prayer3+prayer4etc.

Save all this as a system file:

> save outfile = 'a:prayer.sys'.

will save everything you need for future use, including the information about missing values, and the recoding.

When you want to get the system file back, get the SPSS prompt and then

>get file = 'a:prayer.sys'.

is all you need to be ready to start computing statistics.

Note that you can't *enter* data into a system file. If you need to add data, get the original data file, modify the data in that, and repeat the steps described above to make a new system file. You can save disc space by using the same system filename as before. This will (of course) get rid of the previous system file with the same name. You *can* compute new variables and modify old ones in a system file, and these changes can be saved using the command

>save outfile = . . .

A4.4 Selecting reliable items in SPSS-PC (-X)

This section tells you how to use the reliability facility in SPSS-PC or -X to select reliable items, in order to form a cohesive scale or measure. The command

>reliability variables = prayer1 to prayer8.

gives Cronbach's alpha. The SPSS output will look something like Table A4.4.

First give the normal reliability command, then give a name to the first subscale and list the variables which contribute to that scale, then the second subscale, and so on:

>reliability variables = prayer1 to prayer8/scale(inst) = prayer1 to prayer4/scale(insp) = prayer5 to prayer8.

Table A4.4 SPSS reliability analysis output.

RELIABILITY ANALYSIS – SCALE (ALL)

1. PRAYER1
2. PRAYER2
3. PRAYER3
4. PRAYER4
5. PRAYER5
6. PRAYER6
7. PRAYER7
8. PRAYER8

RELIABILITY COEFFICIENTS

N OF CASES = 80   N OF ITEMS = 8

ALPHA = .7737

Table A4.5 SPSS reliability analysis output (subscales).

RELIABILITY ANALYSIS - SCALE (INST)

1. PRAYER1
2. PRAYER2
3. PRAYER3
4. PRAYER4

RELIABILITY COEFFICIENTS

N OF CASES = 80   N OF ITEMS = 4
ALPHA = .8545

RELIABILITY ANALYSIS - SCALE (INSP)

1. PRAYER5
2. PRAYER6
3. PRAYER7
4. PRAYER8

RELIABILITY COEFFICIENTS

N OF CASES = 80   N OF ITEMS = 4
ALPHA = .6093

The output would give Cronbach's alpha for the subscales comprised of the specified variables, as illustrated in Table A4.5.

The top line tells you that the scale being analyzed involves *all* the items. The items are then listed. The number of cases (subjects) and number of items in the scale are also given. Under the heading "reliability coefficients", only one type of coefficient (alpha) appears, though you could ask for others. This is done by typing, at the *end* of the command for the reliability analysis, the following addition:

>(reliability etc.)/model split.

This will generate split-half reliabilities. You can also ask for Guttman coefficients or other options: consult your menus or handbook.

Improving reliability

Reliability is improved by looking at the item–total correlations of each item, and rejecting those with low item–total correlations. To get item–total correlations you enter:

>reliability variables = prayer1 to prayer8/summary = total.

(For the subscales you would simply enter the variables comprising the subscales, instead of all the variables in the scale).

An output is illustrated in Table A4.6.

Look at the column headed "corrected item-total correlation". This tells you how well the item correlates with the others. If you look in

Table A4.6 SPSS reliability analysis output (item analysis).

ITEM-TOTAL STATISTICS

	SCALE MEAN IF ITEM DELETED	SCALE VARIANCE IF ITEM DELETED	CORRECTED ITEM- TOTAL CORRELATION	ALPHA IF ITEM DELETED
PRAYER1	21.0875	19.7771	.7005	.7151
PRAYER2	20.2875	19.2707	.6359	.7204
PRAYER3	20.5875	20.1188	.6800	.7198
PRAYER4	20.6875	19.4834	.4548	.7568
PRAYER5	20.9875	19.2783	.5799	.7297
PRAYER6	19.3000	26.3392	−.1022	.8307
PRAYER7	20.4875	19.9239	.4384	.7587
PRAYER8	20.2875	21.7264	.6118	.7382

the output in the table, you see that the lowest item–total correlations are for items 4, 6 and 7. Item 6 should certainly go, and we might consider throwing out 4 and 7. Correlations of the order of 0.15 or less could definitely mean the death sentence for any item, unless you are desperately short of higher correlations. The column headed "alpha if item deleted" tells you what the alpha coefficient would be if that item were got rid of. As you can see, the effect of throwing out the less cohesive items is to raise alpha, and vice versa. The first two columns tell you what would happen to the scale mean and variance if each item were deleted.

If you have subscales you should look at item–total correlations as described above, and decide which if any items should be discarded. You can "throw out" items with unsatisfactory item–total correlations, and finish your computing as follows:

> reliability variables = (list the "good" items only e.g.)prayer1 to prayer3 prayer5 prayer8/summary = means.

This gives Cronbach's alpha and descriptive statistics for your final scale. However, the means and ranges are given as for individual items. If you want to compute total scores on your final scale, and find the overall scale mean, range and standard deviation, then first compute the total score by adding the individual item scores:

> compute total = prayer1+prayer2+prayer3+prayer5+prayer8.

To compute overall scale mean and other statistics (norms), use:

> descr var = total.

You may prefer to divide the mean by the number of items in the scale, to give an *item mean*. The advantage of this is that you could then vary the number of items in the scale, and comparisons with the item mean would still make some sense. For the subscales, use the same commands, listing the "good" variables in the subscales. The output would list the items still in the scale or subscale, the number of cases, and the mean, range, and variance of the scale, and the scale and item alphas.

Section 4.2.2 in Chapter 4 suggests procedures to be followed if reliability coefficients are unsatisfactory.

A4.5 Factor and principal components analyses in SPSS-PC (-X)

Factor analysis is a method of examining associations between associations. It finds a small number of underlying dimensions from a larger number of variables, by consolidating the variance. In the case of a test or scale, it will enable you to group items that seem to be assessing the same "factor", by examining the "loading" of all items on each factor, and selecting those with high loadings.

Factor analysis proceeds by first extracting factors, and then if more than one factor emerges, a rotation is carried out to give a clearer picture. Principal components analysis is not actually factor analysis (it uses regression analysis), but it usually gives similar answers and is often used instead of factor analysis. In fact, SPSS does a principal components analysis as the default option in factor analysis.

The command is:

> factor var = prayer1 to prayer8

In spite of the command "factor", this command will cause SPSS to use the default option and to do a principal components analysis, not a true factor analysis. The default option gives a method of rotation called varimax.

You are supposed to have at least three times as many subjects as variables to get a meaningful result from factor or principal components analysis, so our hypothetical prayer example qualifies. Another warning is that if you try to do a factor or principal components analysis on a PC, there may not be enough memory space. The output is quite plentiful.

Eigenvalues

The *eigenvalue* of a factor or principal component indicates how much variance (in the original variables) is accounted for. The convention is to discount factors or principal components with eigenvalues of less than 1. If there is more than one factor (with an eigenvalue greater than 1), then the factors have to be rotated, and a rotated factor matrix will appear. The crucial bits are shown below.

There will be more to the output than described, but there should be sufficient of the important features of factor analysis. The first table that appears is entitled Initial Statistics: it tells you about the factors that have been extracted. Look out for the columns headed

Eigenvalue and Pct of Var. Both express how much of the variance in the original data is accounted for by each of the factors or components extracted (and rotated).

Factors with eigenvalues of less than 1 are not considered meaningful and will not be considered further. The percentage of variance explained by each factor tells you how important that factor is (statistically). In our hypothetical prayer example, three factors were extracted with an eigenvalue greater than 1, between them accounting for 85 per cent of the variance.

If the next part of the output is called factor matrix, it can be ignored if there is more than one factor. If there is only one factor, then it tells you the correlations or "factor loadings" between each variable and the factor, i.e. how much that variable contributes to the factor. Something misleadingly called "final statistics" may appear at this point. It can be ignored.

If there is more than one factor with an eigenvalue greater than 1, then the factors have to be rotated, and a rotated factor matrix will appear. A method called varimax will have been used. This crucial bit of output shows loadings for each variable on each factor. It should look something like Table A4.7.

Interpreting factor loadings and naming factors
This process involves looking at which items have high loadings (above about 0.4) on each factor, deciding what they have in common, and finding a plausible name for each factor in the light of this. Those factors which account for small amounts of variance may be

Table A4.7 SPSS Factor and Principal Components Analysis: part of the output.

Rotated factor matrix

	FACTOR 1	FACTOR 2	FACTOR 3
PRAYER1	.66703	.36674	.54958
PRAYER2	.91230	.19989	.01013
PRAYER3	.51664	.47963	.53758
PRAYER4	.81455	−.06658	−.08590
PRAYER5	.15345	.75830	.46161
PRAYER6	.11349	.06536	−.91070
PRAYER7	−.07708	.96110	.01653
PRAYER8	.28013	.81468	−.09966

dropped. (What constitutes "small" can vary somewhat, but this would normally be below about 8–10 per cent of variance.)

This particular example shows that all the variables behaved as we might have hoped from the results of our reliability analysis. Factor 1 looks like "instrumental prayer" and factor 2 looks like "inspirational prayer", while factor 3 features the recalcitrant item 6. This would confirm the view that only one item (6) need be dropped, and we would be left with a full scale (favourability towards prayer) of all items except 6, and two subscales: instrumental prayer (items 1–4) and inspirational prayer (items 5, 7, 8).

A4.6 Reliability, factor and principal components analyses in SPSS for Windows

Retrieve data if necessary. Select File/Open/Data. Type the filename in the dialogue box (e.g. a: prayer.sav).

Reliability

Select Statistics/Scale/Reliability Analysis.

Enter all items in your scale (or subscale) into the [items] box. Select from the box on the left, click, and click on the right-pointing arrow. This will enter the selected items into the [items] box.

Select required model. As discussed, the default option, Alpha, should normally be run.

Select OK.

The output will resemble those shown in Appendix 4.4.

Factor and principal components analyses

Select Statistics/Data Reduction/Factor.

Enter all items in your scale into the [variables] box. Select from the box on the left, click, and click on the right-pointing arrow. This will enter the selected items into the [variables] box.

Select required options (West 1991 provides a brief guide; Tabachnick & Fidell 1989 has a more elaborate one). Otherwise, a principal components analysis will be carried out by default; this may be your best option.

Select OK.

The output will resemble that shown in Appendix 4.5.

A4.7 Reliability, factor and principal components analyses in CSS

Reliability

Move the cursor down the main display in the Main Menu to O (run Other module), and press "enter".

Select CSS.REL and press "enter".

To retrieve your datafile, press Shift + F1, type in your filename (e.g. a:prayer.dat) and press "enter".

Select the variables to be entered in the reliability analysis: press V, enter the desired variables (e.g. prayer1, prayer2 etc.) and press "enter".

To start the analysis, press "enter" (again).

A menu for reviewing and saving the correlation matrix will appear. This matrix shows the correlations between each item and each other item, and you do not normally need to look at it (if you do need it, follow the menu instructions) – press "enter".

The menu Reliability Results will appear. The screen gives the first descriptive statistics for your scale, but unless your scale is already sufficiently reliable, you don't need these yet. Look at *Cronbach's alpha*. If alpha is high enough (at least over 0.7, preferably over 0.8) you may decide to keep the scale as it is. Print or note the descriptive statistics on the screen (mean, standard deviation, range). If alpha is too low (below 0.7), press F3 to look at item–total correlations. Note those items with low item–total correlations (in the example discussed in Appendix 4 above, these were items 4 and 7). Press "esc" to return to the CSS: Reliability menu, press V to select the variables with the *high* item–total correlations (those to be retained in the scale), and enter these variables. For example, if items prayer1, prayer2, prayer3, prayer5, prayer8 had high item–total correlations and were to be retained, enter those variables, omitting prayer4, prayer6 and prayer7. Press "enter" to compute the new reliability and descriptive statistics.

To compute reliability coefficients other than alpha: press "esc" to return to the CSS reliability menu and select the desired option (e.g. S for split-half reliability), and then proceed as described for alpha.

Factor and principal components analysis

In the Main Menu, move the cursor to F (Factor Analysis/Principal) and press "enter"

Retrieve your data file: press Shift+F1, type in the name of the data file and press "enter"

Press V to bring up the variable list, select the desired variables (e.g. prayer1, prayer2 etc.) and press "enter".

The next menu allows you to select various options in calculating the correlation matrix, which is the first step in factor and principal components analyses. If you are interested, consult the handbook for more details. Normally, however, just press "enter" to continue. The next menu allows you to display the matrix showing correlations between each item and each other item, to save this matrix, and to pursue various other options. Normally, however, press "enter" to continue. The next menu allows you to choose the method of estimating the communalities – amount of variance accounted for. Normally, however, the default option may be followed, which is principal components analysis, so press "enter" to continue.

Press "enter" twice more to continue the analysis. A menu headed Analysis should appear. To see communalities (amount of variance accounted for): select V, press "enter" and press N. Record or save desired information about communalities, and press "esc" to return to the Analysis menu.

From the Analysis menu, select R. A Rotation menu should appear, with various options. Normally, you should try a varimax rotation: press V, press "enter" twice, and then once more to accept the next default option. Finally, press L and then T to give factors and factor loadings.

To interpret factor loadings (as stated in Appendix 4.5) look at which items have high loadings (above about 0.4) on each factor, decide what they have in common, and dream up a plausible name for each factor in the light of this. Factors which account for small amounts of variance may be dropped. (What constitutes "small" can vary somewhat, but this would normally be below about 8–10 per cent of variance.)

A4.8 For those without a reliability facility

Alternative ways of doing reliability statistics are available.

A4.8.1 Basic method for examining scale cohesiveness

First calculate for each subject a preliminary total score. This score indicates how "high" or "low" each subject reports their self to be on whatever you are assessing. If you have some "negatively worded" items, you will need to reverse their scores before calculating this preliminary total.

For example, consider the example from Chapter 2, the questionnaire on prayer. Answers from a hypothetical subject have been written in at the end of each item below.

Write a number next to each of the following statements to show how much you agree with it:

5 = strongly agree
4 = agree somewhat
3 = uncertain or neutral
2 = disagree somewhat
1 = strongly disagree

1. It is important to pray when you need help.2
2. Prayer is a waste of time.5 reverse = 1
3. Praying gives comfort.3
4. It is foolish to believe that prayers get answered.4 reverse = 2
   etc.

A high score on this test will indicate agreement with beliefs about the positive benefits of prayer. Items 2 and 4 are negatively worded, so you need to reverse the scoring for these items as follows:

change 5 to 1
4 to 2
2 to 4
1 to 5
leave 3 unchanged.

In the example above, this makes the answer to item 2 become 1, and to item 4 become 2. (If answers to these questions had just been yes/no, then you would score 1 for a yes, 0 for a no, and vice versa for negatively worded items). Now add up all the numbers. For just the items given above, the total for the subject shown is 8. The hypothetical minimum score on those 4 items is 5, and the maximum is 20, so the subject's answers suggest fairly low agreement with beliefs about the positive benefits of prayer. Produce a preliminary total score for each subject.

Secondly, carry out *item analysis* to examine the *cohesiveness (internal consistency, reliability)* of your scale. (There are other ways of assessing reliability, such as split-half reliability and test–retest reliability.) The basic idea is to find those items that correlate best with total scores on the scale. Those that do can be retained as cohesive items, and those that do not can be discarded.

Finally, select the items with highest item–total correlations. Subjects can be rescored on this final scale, and norms shown (means, standard deviations and description of the people tested).

A4.8.2 A method for doing item–total correlations

This method uses a statistics package which will do correlations.
1. Make a data file, entering subjects' responses to your scale/test items as described in Appendix 4.3
2. Check it for accuracy.
3. Reverse the scoring of any items, where necessary.
4. Compute a (preliminary) total on the scale.
5. Correlate the responses to each item, in turn, with the total (item–total correlation).
6. Select those with the highest (preferably statistically significant) correlations.
7. These form your new, reliable, cohesive questionnaire. You do not have to administer it again. You can just recompute new total scores on these items alone.
8. Compute means and standard deviations on the final scale/test.

A4.8.3 A method for examining scale cohesiveness for those without access to computing facilities

This method involves simplifying the data somewhat, in the interests of feasibility.
1. Calculate a (preliminary) total score for each subject.
2. Group the subjects into two halves, one half "high-scorers" (total preliminary scores above the median), and the other half "low-scorers" (total preliminary scores below the median).
3. Look at each answer to each item in turn and decide whether it is an "agree", neutral, or "disagree". For this purpose you can ignore differences such as that between "strongly agree" and "agree somewhat". Ignore the neutral answers.
4. Construct, for each item, a 2×2 contingency table showing the numbers of subjects with high total scores who agreed with the item, the numbers of high-scorers who disagreed, and so on, as shown in Table A4.8.

You should have as many tables as there are items in your test. Examine each of the contingency tables. If one row has zero or very

Table A4.8 A contingency table.

	High total	Low total
Agree	8	2
Disagree	3	6

Table A4.9 A contingency table that would be obtained for an item with which most people agreed.

	High total	Low total
Agree	8	9
Disagree	2	0

Table A4.10 A contingency table that would be obtained for an item which related poorly to other items.

	High total	Low total
Agree	5	4
Disagree	4	6

low frequencies, that item can be discarded: everyone or nearly agreed or disagreed with it, and it is not discriminating between people. Table A4.9 shows an example.

If the frequencies look fairly evenly distributed across the four cells, then that item can also be discarded, as there is no relationship between that item and answers to other items. Table A4.10 shows an example.

If, however, there seems to be a tendency for high-scorers to agree (*or* disagree) with the item, and vice versa for low scorers, then there is some association between answers to the item under scrutiny and answers to other items on the test. This was the case with the first example (Table A4.8).

Carry out a Fisher Exact test (if numbers are small) or a chi-square (if numbers are sufficiently large). Note that significance levels for the Fisher Exact Test can be looked up directly from tables such as those in Siegel & Castellan (1988) and no calculations other than very simple addition are required.

5. Select those items which showed a significant association with the (preliminary) total scores on the scale. These items form the new, cohesive scale.
6. Calculate a new total for each subject on the new scale, and calculate norms (means, standard deviations).

Appendix to Chapter 5

Validity and related statistics

In these appendices full instructions are given for carrying out the necessary statistical tests for the main types of validity, using SPSS-PC (and -X). Briefer instructions are given for SPSS for Windows and for CSS, and if you are using these, you may occasionally find helpful the fuller explanations given along with SPSS-PC, especially in understanding the output.

A5.1 Criterion validity: t-test (SPSS-PC or SPSS-X)

Here is how to use SPSS (-PC and -X) to examine the scores of two groups on your measure for significant differences. If you have not computed each person's total score on your measure, the SPSS command is:

> compute total = prayer1 + prayer2 + prayer3 + prayer4 + prayer5 + prayer7 + prayer8.

You simply ask SPSS to add the scores on all the items in your final scale. You can also compute totals for your subscales, e.g. if it had been decided to look at belief in the worth of instrumental prayer (inst), the command to compute the subscale would be:

> compute inst = prayer1 + prayer2 + prayer3 + prayer4.

Total scores can be saved as described in Appendix 4.3. Now carry out the t-test, using the following command:

> t-test groups = relig(0,1)/var = total.

Table A5.1 SPSS t-test output.

Group 1: relig eq .00
Group 2: relig eq 1.00
t-test for: TOTAL

	Number of cases	Mean	Standard deviation	Standard error
Group 1	32	11.5000	3.331	.589
Group 2	48	15.1667	3.168	.457

Pooled variance estimate				Separate variance estimate			
F value	2-tail prob	t value	Degrees of freedom	2-tail prob	t value	Degrees of freedom	2-tail prob
1.11	.737	-4.97	78	.000	-4.92	64.20	.000

In the "groups" bit of the command put the variable name of the groups to be compared (it was called "relig" in our example), and then in brackets the values on that variable. For a t-test, there should be only two values. (If you have more than two groups, then you should do an analysis of variance using the method described in Appendix 5.4). In the "variable" bit of the command, you name the dependent variable you want: it could be one of your subscales. A sample t-test output is shown in Table A5.1.

The first two lines tell you that group 1 consists of all those for whom "relig" was 0, i.e. the non-affiliated, and that group 2 was those for whom "relig" was 1, i.e. the affiliated. This is the independent variable. The third line tells you what the dependent variable was in this analysis. Here it was subject's total scores on the prayer measure. Next is a little table telling you what the mean scores (and standard deviations and errors) were for the two groups, on the prayer measure. The column to attend to is the one headed "mean". You can see that group 2's mean is higher that group 1's.

Was the difference statistically significant? (What was the probability of observing those differences by chance?) The first two columns in the table at the bottom tell you whether you should be looking for your answer among the columns headed "Pooled variance estimate" or "Separate variance estimate". The traditional t-test (based on a pooled variance estimate) assumes homogeneity of variance, and the first two columns at the bottom of the SPSS output give the results of a test for homogeneity of variance. If the two groups have similar variances you should look for the t value based on a pooled variance estimate. If the two groups have non-homogeneous variance (i.e. they

have significantly different variances) then t needs to be based on separate variance estimates. So the rule is:
- if the first probability value is more than 0.05, look at the first t-value (pooled variance)
- if the first probability value is less than 0.05, look at the second t-value (separate variance).

In the example above, the first probability value was greater than 0.05, the variances of the two groups were homogeneous, and therefore the first value of t (4.97) should be taken.

Sometimes t appears with a minus sign. You do not usually have to take account of this. It just indicates the direction of the difference between the groups, which is something you should have your eye on anyway.

You should concern yourself with the question of one- or two-tailed probabilities. If you have predicted the *direction* of the difference between two groups, then you should take the one-tailed probability – assuming that you observed a difference in the predicted direction. In the present case, the difference between the two groups was predicted, so a one-tailed probability should be used. This is obtained by dividing the quoted two-tailed probability by 2.

A5.2 Concurrent and predictive validity: entering new data (SPSS-PC and SPSS-X)

This section is likely to be needed only if you have no experience of adding more data to an existing database. It applies mainly to those working with SPSS-PC and SPSS-X (Appendix 4.3. explains how to proceed with SPSS for Windows and with CSS).

Call up your database (but *not* your system file, if you have one). If it was made using DOS as described in Appendix 4.3, then the command would be:

> edit filename.

Enter the new data for each subject, for example their answers to the items of a test. Reverse the scoring of items where necessary (use the recode command). Compute total scores on the test (use the compute command). Alternatively, you could work out subjects' scores on the test by hand, and just enter these total scores on to your database. However, it is usually quicker to do the scoring by computer. Save the new form of the data file (using the same filename as before, which will get rid of your old data file and reduce unnecessary clutter on your disc). Check the new data entered. For example, get into SPSS and carry out the checks described in Section 4.1. You can then make a system file if you wish (see Appendix 4.3). The command is:

>save outfile = 'filename.sys'.

You use the same system filename as before: the older file with that name will be replaced, saving disc space. Note that a system file should have a different name from the original database from which it was derived, otherwise the original database will be replaced by the system file, and hence lost. It does not matter what you call them, but a useful convention is to call databases: filename.dat and system files could be called filename.sys.

A5.3 Concurrent validity: using SPSS-PC or SPSS-X to calculate correlations

Concurrent validity generally involves looking at the correlation between scores on your new scale and scores on a standard scale. Get into SPSS and either get your system file (the command is: get file = 'filename') or, use the data list file command to get your data file, and then use the missing values, recode and compute commands to compute the total score on your scale if you have not already done this. Correlations are obtained by:

>corr total standard

(where total is the score on your test, and standard is the score on the standard test). A sample output is shown in Table A5.2.

This tells you the names of the variables being correlated, the correlations with each other (this information is repeated, so just ignore the duplication) and the level of statistical significance. Here, a minus sign by the correlation means a *negative* association between the

Table A5.2 SPSS correlation output.

Correlations:	TOTAL	STANDARD
TOTAL	1.0000	.4517**
STANDARD	.4517**	1.0000
N of cases: 80	1-tailed signif: * - .01 ** - .001	

variables (high values on one go with low values on the other). Note that this output tells you one-tailed significance levels. With this output, if you had *not* predicted the direction of association (unlikely in the case of validity testing), you should check statistical tables to find the significance levels of the obtained correlation coefficients, because you would need two-tailed significance levels.

A5.4 Criterion and predictive validity: one-way analysis of variance in SPSS (including comparisons)

If you are comparing *scores* on your measure with *scores* on some other measure, you should carry out correlations, as described in Appendix 5.3. If, however, you are looking at scores on your measure in relation to "group membership" (a discontinuous, categorical variable, such as whether people belong to group A, B or C, or performed behaviour X, Y or Z) – then you need to carry out either a t-test (see Appendix 5.1) or an analysis of variance (anova). An (unrelated) t-test can be done when comparing scores of two groups, while anova is needed for more than two groups, and for more complex research designs outside the scope of this book.

As an aside, in terms of statistical theory, there is nothing really wrong with doing an anova to look for differences between scores of two groups, and the anova is just as "sensitive" as the t-test. An interesting historical note is that the t-test was introduced to help novices, working with simple two-group comparisons; in pre-computer days it was easier to calculate t than to do an anova.

To do a one-way anova in SPSS, use the following command:

> oneway total by grpname (0,2).

"Grpname" is whatever you have decided to call your performance measure, which you are using as a grouping variable. In the brackets put the highest and lowest values on that variable. They do not have to be "higher" or "lower" than each other: they can be categories which are not ordered. In our prayer example, we might have information on whether students who did the test joined one of two religious groups on campus, or joined no group. We could call this variable "religrp" and code the three possibilities 0, 1 and 2 but the numbers do not indicate anything about their ordering. A sample output is shown in Table A5.3.

Table A5.3   SPSS anova (one-way) output.

ANALYSIS OF VARIANCE
TOTAL
By RELIGRP

Source	D.F.	Sum of squares	Mean squares	F	F sign
Main effects	2	614.13	307.07	51.55	.000
Religrp	2	614.13	307.07	51.55	.000
Explained	2	614.13	307.07	51.55	.000
Residual	77	448.67	5.957		
Total	79	1072.80	13.580		

One reason that this output appears to be repeating information is that it is a format which can deal with more complicated analyses of variance – involving two or more grouping variables. In that case, the top three rows of figures would not normally be identical. To look at the relation between scores on the prayer measure, and religious-group-joining ("religrp") we look at the row of figures next to the source of variance we are interested in: the grouping variable, i.e. religrp. Ignore the columns headed "sum of squares" and "mean squares", and look at the F ratio and the significance level. You also need to quote the degrees of freedom associated with F ratio, which are the degrees of freedom for the source of variance examined (in this case 2) and the degrees of freedom for the residual variance, sometimes called the "error" (in this case 77). Degrees of freedom are written as: $F_{2,77} = \ldots$

To present the results of an analysis of variance, you need to present an analysis of variance table if there was a fairly complex research design involving two or more grouping variables (the note at the end of this section mentions the command to be used in such a case) and/or a mixed analysis of variance involving within-subjects and between-subjects effects. In a case with only one grouping variable, an anova table is not necessary; you need to focus on only one F ratio, and the results can be presented by quoting the F ratio, the two relevant figures for degrees of freedom, and the probability. Thus our example would be:

Significant differences in prayer scores went with later religious-group-joining: $F_{2,77} = 51.55$, p = 0.000.

You should also use the command:

>means total by religrp.

The output will tell you the means associated with each group and enable you to see where the differences lie. These means should be quoted in presenting results. Supposing the means for the three groups tested were:

2.77, 5.69, 5.89.

You need to be able to state which of those means were different from each other. Here you have to ask for comparisons to be made. You might have been confident before you did your testing that the two groups of people who joined campus religious organizations were going to score similarly, and higher than those not joining a religious organization. But you might not have been sure whether the two groups joining religious organizations were going to have similar or different scores.

If you predicted differences between groups, then *planned comparisons* need to be asked for. Follow the method described by West (1991). If you had not been certain about predicted differences, then you can use *post-hoc (unplanned) comparisons*. Scheffe's (1953) method is normally used. An advantage of doing *post hoc*, unplanned comparisons, compared to planned comparisons, is that SPSS tries all possible comparisons between individual groups for you, whereas doing planned contrasts in SPSS involves a tedious process of writing out a long command for the contrasts to be made. The advantages of planned comparisons are that you are more likely to detect differences (attain statistical significance), and you can also pool together groups to show up salient differences (for example groups 1 and 2 versus group 0 in the example below).

The command for unplanned comparisons in SPSS would be in the following form:

>oneway total by grpname (0,2)/ranges = scheffe(.05).

The (.05) tells SPSS to indicate between which groups there is a difference significant at $p < 0.05$ or better. You can specify (0.01) if you want to be stricter, or any other level of significance desired. The output will include a grid looking like Table A5.4. (If you are initially puzzled by the rows of Gs, rs and ps, try reading them from top to bottom: they are "Grp", an abbreviation for "group".)

The asterisks show which groups were significantly different from

Table 5.4 SPSS output for unplanned contrasts.

Variable TOTAL

		G G G
		r r r
		P P P
Mean	Group	0 1 2
2.7655	Grp 0	
5.6911	Grp 1	*
5.8878	Grp 2	*

which other groups in the *post hoc* comparison. A further part of the output (not shown) arranges the groups into subsets whose highest and lowest means do not differ by more than the shortest significant range for a subset of that size. In the example, groups 1 and 2 do not differ significantly from each other, but both differ significantly from group 0.

Note that if you were doing an analysis of variance with *two or more independent or grouping variables*, the command would be:

>anova total by grpname1 (0,2) grpname2 (0,1).)

A5.5 T-tests, anovas and correlations in SPSS for Windows

This section briefly describes the SPSS for Windows procedures for obtaining the statistics you are likely to need in examining the validity of your scale. Remember that if you cannot see the part of the output that you need, you can use the arrow keys to scroll the output up or down.

If you have not got your data file in action, you should first retrieve your data file using the procedure described in Appendix 4.3.1, using the File/Open/Data selection. If you have not yet computed total scores on your scale (and any subscales), select Transform. A dialogue box should appear. In the Target Variable box, type a name for the variable you are computing (e.g. total).

The box headed Numeric Expression needs to be filled with the variables to be used in the computation, and the appropriate mathematical operators. Click on the first chosen variable in the left-hand list, click on the right-pointing arrow next to the list, and then click on the appropriate mathematical operator (selected from the area that looks like the key-pad of a calculator) until you have completed the formula. For example

prayer1 + prayer2 + prayer3 + prayer4 + prayer5 +prayer6 + prayer7 + prayer8.

Click on OK. This computed total may be saved in your data file using the method described in Appendix 4.3.1.

T-tests
Select Statistics/Compare Means/Independent Samples T Test. A dialogue box should appear. Insert variable(s) to be compared in the Test Variables window (e.g. total). Select the chosen variable, click, then select the right-pointing arrow by the Test Variable window, and click. Insert the grouping variable name in the Grouping Variable window (e.g. relig). Select the chosen variable, click, then select the right-pointing arrow by the Grouping Variable window, and click. Click Define Groups. In the dialogue box, enter the values on the grouping variable defining the two groups to be compared. If we use the example from Appendix 5.1, with religious affiliation (relig) as the grouping variable: insert the value 0 for Group 1, move the cursor to the group 2 window, click, and enter the value 1 for Group 2. Click on Continue. Click on OK.

The output is similar to that shown in Appendix 5.1, except that the F-value may be labelled Levene's Test for Equality of Variance, or Test for Homogeneity of Variance. You use this F value to decide which of the two t-values shown you should use. If the F-value shows that the two groups have equal variances (i.e. $p > 0.05$) then you should take the t-value from the row entitled "equal". If the F-value shows that the two groups have unequal variances ($p < 0.05$), then you should use the t-value from the row entitled "unequal". Secondly, the output also gives standard errors and 95 per cent confidence intervals (CI) for the difference between the two groups.

Analysis of variance
Select Statistics/Compare Means/One-Way Anova. A dialogue box should appear. Enter the dependent variable (e.g. total) in the Dependent List box. Select the variable from the list on the left, click, move the cursor to the right-pointing arrow next to the dependent variable window, and click. Enter the grouping (independent) variable (e.g. religrp) into the Factor box. Select the variable from the list

125

on the left, click, move the cursor to the right-pointing arrow next to the Factor window, and click. Click on the Define Range button. In the box that appears you enter the lowest value on your grouping (independent variable) (e.g. 0) in the Minimum box, move the cursor to the Maximum box, click, and enter the highest value (e.g. 2) in the Maximum box. Select Continue and click.

To get the means and other descriptive statistics for each group being compared, select Options from the One-Way Anova box, and check Descriptive from the Statistics area. Click on Continue. To check whether the groups being compared have homogeneous variance, select Options from the One-Way Anova box, and check Levene, or homogeneity of variance. Click on Continue.

To do *post hoc* comparisons of differences between individual means, click on the Post Hoc button in the One-Way Anova box, and select the preferred test (e.g. Scheffe). If you had made predictions about differences, follow the method described in Foster (1993). Click on OK. The output is similar to that given in Appendix 5.4.

Two-way analyses of variance may be done by selecting Statistics/ ANOVA Models/Simple Factorial. The procedure is similar to that described above, except that you enter two grouping (independent) variables in the Factor box, and define the ranges of both.

Correlations
Select Statistics/Correlate/Bivariate. A dialogue box should appear. Insert variables to be analyzed: move cursor to desired variables, click, move cursor to right-pointing arrow next to variables box, and click. Select required correlation coefficients by checking the relevant alternatives in Correlation Coefficients area. Usually this would be Pearson. If, however, data are discontinuous, but ordinal, then select Kendall or Spearman. Click on OK. The output is similar to the SPSS-PC output illustrated in Appendix 5.3. The main difference is that in SPSS for Windows, $p < 0.05$ is represented by a single asterisk (*), and $p < 0.01$ by a double asterisk (**).

To print results
Select File/Print/OK.

A5.6 T-tests, anovas and correlations in CSS

This section briefly describes the CSS procedures for obtaining the statistics you are likely to need in examining the validity of your scale. The examples given are from the hypothetical prayer questionnaire and scale described in Appendix 4, where the variable names for the scale items are prayer1, prayer2, etc.

To compute total scores on your refined scale, first retrieve your data file: press Shift+F1, type in the filename and press "enter". Now select d (data management) and then t (data transformation/recodes). Press Y: a screen headed Transformation should appear. Type in a name for the variable to be computed (e.g. total), select the variables (e.g. prayer1, prayer2, prayer3, prayer5, prayer8) *by typing the number next to each variable* and then pressing "enter", and the arithmetic operator required (addition). Press "enter". Save the computed variable (total) by pressing "esc", enter D and press "enter".

T-tests
Select B (Basic Statistics) from the main menu and press "enter". A menu headed "Basic Statistics" should appear. Retrieve your data file (if you have not yet done this): press Shift+F1, type in the filename (e.g. a:religion.dat) and press "enter". Select I (t-test for independent samples). Press "enter".

Specify the independent (grouping) variable: press I (for independent variable) and then enter the variable *by typing the number next to the required variable* (e.g. relig) and pressing "enter". Now specify the values on the independent/grouping variable e.g. 0 and 1, by pressing 0, followed by "enter", and 1, followed by "enter".

Specify the dependent variable(s) to be compared. Press Q (dependent variables) and select the desired variables. Remember to do this by typing in the number next to required variable (e.g. total, the computed total of scores on your refined scale) and pressing "enter".

Press "enter" again to compute. The results can be scrolled up and down if necessary. A two-tailed T, probability, numbers of cases, and means for each group will be displayed. The probability can be halved if you had predicted the direction of differences between the two groups (i.e. predicted which group would score higher than the other).

Analysis of variance (anova)

Select A (Quick Anova) from the main menu. Press "enter". A menu headed Quick Anova/Ancova should appear. Retrieve your data file (if you have not yet done so): press Shift+F1, type in the filename (e.g. a:prayer.dat) and press "enter".

Press I (independent variables) and select desired independent/ grouping variable(s) (e.g. religrp) by typing the number next to the variable(s) desired and pressing "enter". Now press C and enter the range of values on each independent/grouping variable, putting a hyphen between the lowest and highest values (e.g. 0-2). Press "enter".

Press D (dependent variables), type in the number next to the desired variable name (e.g. total), and press "enter". Press "enter" (again) to start the anova.

The output menu enables you to select an anova table, means and standard deviations, planned or *post hoc* comparisons. All of these are either necessary or very useful.

Correlations

Select B (basic statistics) from the main menu, and press "enter". Select C (correlations) from the basic statistics menu. Retrieve your data file (if you have not yet done so): press Shift+F1, type in the filename (e.g. a:prayer.dat) and press "enter". Press Q (correlation matrix).

Select variables to be correlated by typing the number next to the desired variables, pressing "enter" after each selection. Press "enter" again, to compute.

The correlation matrix can be viewed by entering C when a menu appears. If you have correlated a large number of variables, the matrix will be large and you will have to scroll using the cursor keys. You can move the highlight to any desired correlation and press F10: this will display the significance (p) of the correlation among other information.

A5.7 Confounded variables: loglinear analysis, logistic regression, analysis of covariance and multiple regression analysis

For more detailed discussion of these methods refer to a more advanced statistics text, and/or statistics software manual. This section simply gives SPSS-PC (and -X) commands and a very brief explanation for the output for each of these methods of analysis. Further options are available, and the manual should be consulted for details.

In all cases

> *IV1 IV2 IV3* refers to the names of the independent (outcome) variable(s) being analyzed
> *DV* refers to the name of the dependent (predictor) variable.

Loglinear analysis

> hiloglin DV (0,1) IV1 (0,1) IV2 (0,1) IV3 (0,1)/print = assoc.

The variables may be specified in any order, and the figures in brackets should be the highest and lowest values of the categorical variables. The output will include partial chi-squares and probabilities for associations between all combinations of variables.

Logistic regression

> logistic regression/variable DV with IV1 IV2 IV3.

The default method is "enter". The output will include Betas and probabilities for the associations between each of the IVs and the DV.

Analysis of covariance

> anova DV by IV1 (0,1) with IV2.

The output will express the "pure" effect of IV1 on the DV (uncontaminated by IV2) by an F ratio (with associated probability), in an anova table.

Multiple regression

> regress var = DV IV1 IV2 IV3/dep = DV/method = enter.

The output will include a T value and probability expressing the strength of the relationship between each of the IVs and the DV.

In SPSS for Windows and CSS, ensure that you know which are the independent (or grouping) variables, which is the dependent (or outcome variable) (and for analysis of covariance, which are the covariate/s). Select the appropriate analysis: use Table 5.1 in Chapter 5 as a guide. Enter the independent and dependent variables. This appendix provides a very brief guide to interpreting the output.

Bibliography

Adorno, T. W., E. Frenkel-Brunswick, D. J. Levinson, R. N. Sanford 1950. *The authoritarian personality*. New York: Harper & Row.

Allport, G. W. & P. E. Vernon 1960. *Study of values*. Boston: Houghton Mifflin.

American Educational Research Association, American Psychological Association, National Council on Measurement in Education 1985. *Standards for educational and psychological tests*. Washington, DC: American Psychological Association.

American Psychiatric Association 1980. *Diagnostic and statistical manual of mental disorders* (DSMIII). Washington, DC: American Psychiatric Association.

American Psychological Association (see American Educational Research Association).

Anastasi, A. 1988. *Psychological testing*, 6th edn. New York: Macmillan.

Arnkoff, D. 1983. Cognitive and specific factors in cognitive therapy. In *Psychotherapy and patient relationships*, M. J. Lambert (ed.). Homewood, Illinois: Dow Jones-Irwin.

Australian Psychological Society 1994. *Code of professional conduct*. POB 126, Carlton South 3053, Victoria, Australia: Australian Psychological Society.

Bartram, D. 1993. *Certificate of competence in occupational testing (level B): discussion paper*. Leicester: British Psychological Society.

Bartram, D. & P. A. A. Lindley 1994. *Psychological testing: The BPS level A open learning programme*. Leicester: British Psychological Society.

Bartram, D., P. A. A. Lindley, J. Foster, L. Marshall 1990. *Review of psychometric tests for assessment in vocational training*. Leicester: BPS Books.

Batson, C. D. 1976. Religion as prosocial: agent or double agent? *Journal for the Scientific Study of Religion* 15, 29–45.

Batson, C. D., P. Schoenrade, W. L. Ventis 1993. *Religion and the individual*. New York & Oxford: Oxford University Press.

131

Beck, A. T. & R. A. Steer 1987. *The Beck Depression Inventory*. San Antonio: The Psychological Corporation/Harcourt Brace Jovanovitch.

Beck, A. T., A. J. Rush, B. F. Shaw, G. Emery 1979. *Cognitive therapy and depression*. New York: Guilford Press.

Bradley, C., D. S. Gamsu, J. L. Moses, G. Knight, A. J. M. Boulton, J. Drury, J. D. Ward 1987. The use of diabetes-specific perceived control and health belief measures to predict treatment choice and efficacy in a feasibility study of continuous subcutaneous insulin infusion pumps. *Psychology and Health* **1**, 133–46.

Brenner, M., J. Brown, D. Canter 1985. *The research interview: uses and approaches*. London: Academic Press.

Brewin, C. R. 1993. Personal communication.

British Psychological Society 1994. *Certificate of competence in occupational testing (Level A): general information pack*. Leicester: British Psychological Society.

British Psychological Society Steering Committee on Test Standards 1992. *Psychological testing: a guide*. Leicester: British Psychological Society.

Brown, G. W. & T. O. Harris 1978. *The social origins of depression*. London: Tavistock.

Brown, L. B. 1994. *The human side of prayer: the psychology of praying*. Birmingham, Alabama: Religious Education Press.

Burns, M. S. A. 1974. Life styles for women: an attitude scale. *Psychological Reports* **35**, 227–30.

Burns, R. B. 1979. *The self-concept in theory, measurement, development and behaviour*. London: Longman.

Buros Institute of Mental Measurement 1992. *The 11th mental measurements yearbook*. J. J. Kramer & J. C. Conoley (eds), L. L. Murphy (managing ed.). Highland Park, New Jersey: Gryphon Press. (Note that earlier editions of the yearbook may be needed to obtain complete information on any given test).

Cattell, R. B. 1946. *Description and measurement of personality*. London: Harrap.

Cattell, R. B. 1965. *The scientific analysis of personality*. Baltimore, Maryland: Penguin.

Cattell, R. B., H. W. Eber, M. M. Tatsuoka 1970. *The Sixteen Personality Factor (16PF) test*. Champaign, Illinois: Institute for Personality and Ability Testing.

Cohen, J. 1988. *Statistical power analysis for the behavioural sciences*, 2nd edn. Hillsdale, New Jersey: Erlbaum.

Cohen, J. 1992. A power primer. *Psychological Bulletin* **112**, 155–9.

Cook, M. 1993. *Levels of personality*. London: Cassell Educational.

Coolican, H. 1990. *Research methods and statistics in psychology*. London: Hodder & Stoughton.

Coopersmith, S. 1967. *The antecedents of self esteem.* San Francisco: Freeman.

Cronbach, L. J. 1951. Coefficient alpha and the interval structure of tests. *Psychometrika* **16**, 297–334.

Crowne, D. & D. Marlowe 1960. A new scale of social desirability independent of psychopathology. *Journal of Consulting Psychology* **24**, 349–54.

Dawidowicz, L. S. 1977. *The Jewish presence: essays on identity and history.* New York: Holt, Rinehart and Winston.

De Vaus, D. A. 1993. *Surveys in social research,* 3rd edn. London: UCL Press.

Dobson, K. S., B. F. Shaw, T. M. Vallis 1985. Reliability of a measure of the quality of cognitive therapy. *British Journal of Clinical Psychology* **24**, 295–300.

Edwards, A. L. 1957. *The social desirability variable in personality assessment and research.* New York: Dryden.

Elliott, C. D. 1983. *The British ability scales.* Slough, England: National Foundation for Educational Research.

Ellis, H. 1898. Auto-eroticism: a psychological study. *Alienist and Neurologist* **19**, 260–99.

Emery, G., S. D. Hollon, R. C. Bedrosian 1981. *New directions in cognitive therapy: a casebook.* New York: Guilford Press.

Emmons, R. A. 1984. Factor analysis and construct validity of the Narcissistic Personality Inventory. *Journal of Personality Assessment* **48**, 291–300.

English, H. B. & A. C. English 1958. *A comprehensive dictionary of psychological and psychoanalytical terms.* New York: Longmans, Green.

Eysenck, H. J. 1952. *The scientific study of personality.* London: Routledge & Kegan Paul.

Eysenck, H. J. & S. B. G. Eysenck 1964. *The Eysenck Personality Inventory.* London: Hodder & Stoughton.

Eysenck, H. J. & S. B. G. Eysenck 1975. *Manual of the Eysenck Personality Questionnaire.* San Diego, California: Edits.

Fitts, W. H. 1955. *Manual Tennessee Department of Mental Health Self-Concept Scale.* Nashville, Tennessee.

Foster, J. J. 1993. *Starting SPSS-PC+ and SPSS for Windows.* Wilmslow, England: Sigma Press.

Franken, I. R. 1988. Sensation seeking, decision making styles, and preference for individual responsibility. *Personality and Individual Differences* **9**, 139–46.

Freud, S. 1914. On narcissism: an introduction. In *The standard edition of the complete psychological works of Sigmund Freud,* J. Strachey (ed. and trans.) Vol. 14 (1957). London: Hogarth Press.

Freud, S. 1923. The ego and the id. In *The standard edition of the complete psychological works of Sigmund Freud*, J. Strachey (ed. and trans.) Vol. 19 (1961). London: Hogarth Press.

Given, C. W., B. A. Given, R. S. Gallin, J. W. Condon 1983. Development of scales to measure beliefs of diabetic patients. *Research in Nursing and Health* 6, 127–41.

Glock, C. Y. & R. Stark 1966. *Christian beliefs and anti-semitism*. New York: Harper & Row.

Glock, C. Y., G. J. Selznick, J. L. Spaeth 1966. *The apathetic majority: a study based on public responses to the Eichmann trial*. New York: Harper & Row.

Glock, C. Y., R. Wuthnow, J. A. Piliavin, M. Spencer 1975. *Adolescent prejudice*. New York: Harper & Row.

Hathaway, S. R. & J. C. McKinley 1951, 1967. *The Minnesota Multiphasic Personality Inventory*. Minneapolis, Minnesota: NCS Interpretive Scoring Systems, University of Minnesota.

Heatherton, T. & J. Polivy 1991. Development and validation of a scale for measuring state self-esteem. *Journal of Personality and Social Psychology* 60, 895–910.

Heim, A. W. 1968. *Group test of high grade intelligence AH5*. Slough, England: National Foundation for Educational Research.

Heim, A. W. 1970. *Group test of general intelligence AH4*. Slough, England: National Foundation for Educational Research.

Heim, A. W., K. P. Watts, V. Simmons 1983. *Group tests of high level intelligence*. Slough, England: National Foundation for Educational Research.

Higginbotham, J. B. & K. K. Cox 1979. *Focus group interviews: a reader*. Chicago: American Marketing Association.

Holmes, T. H. & R. H. Rahe 1967. The social readjustment rating scale. *Journal of Psychosomatic Research* 11, 213–18.

Hood, R. W. Jr 1975. The construction and preliminary validation of a measure of reported mystical experience. *Journal for the Scientific Study of Religion* 14, 29–41.

Institute of Personnel Management 1993. IPM *code on psychological testing*. London: Institute of Personnel Management.

Jenkins, C. D., S. J. Zyzanski, R. H. Rosenman 1978. Coronary-prone behaviour: one pattern or several? *Psychosomatic Medicine* 40, 25–43.

Jenkins, C. D., S. J. Zyzanski, R. H. Rosenman 1979. *Jenkins Activity Survey Form C: Manual*. San Antonio: The Psychological Corporation/ Harcourt Brace Jovanovitch.

Johnson, C. & S. Blinkhorn 1994. Desperate measures: job performance and personality test measures. *The Psychologist* 7, 167–70.

Jung, C. G. 1923. *Psychological types*. New York: Harcourt.

Kanner, A. D., J. C. Coyne, C. Schaefer, R. S. Lazarus 1981. Comparison of two modes of stress measurement: daily hassles and uplifts versus major life events. *Journal of Behavioural Medicine* **4**, 1–39.

Kendall, I., J. Jenkinson, M. de Lemos, D. Clancy 1994. *The Australian Psychological Society Limited: supplement to guidelines for the use of psychological tests.* POB 126, Carlton South 3053, Victoria, Australia: Australian Psychological Society.

Kish, L. 1965. *Survey sampling.* New York: Wiley.

Kline, P. 1986. *A handbook of test construction.* London: Methuen.

Kline, P. 1993. *The handbook of psychological testing.* London: Routledge.

Krueger, R. A. 1994. *Focus groups: a practical guide for applied research.* London: Sage.

Levinson, H. 1973. Activism and powerful others: distinction within the concept of internal-external control. *Journal of Personality Assessment* **38**, 377–83.

Likert, R. A. 1932. A technique for the measurement of attitudes. *Archives of Psychology* 40–53.

McCracken, G. 1988. *The long interview.* Newbury Park, California: Sage.

Marx, G. T. 1967. *Protest and prejudice: a study of belief in the Black community.* New York: Harper & Row.

Maton, K. 1989. The stress-buffering role of spiritual support. *Journal for the Scientific Study of Religion* **28**, 310–23.

Medical Research Council 1992. *Responsibility in investigations on human participants and material on personal information.* London: Medical Research Council.

Melzack, R. 1975. The McGill Pain Questionnaire: major properties and scoring methods. *Pain* **1**, 277–99.

Morgan, D. L. 1988. *Focus groups as qualitative research.* London: Sage.

Myers, I. B. & M. H. McCaulley 1985. *A guide to the development and use of the Myers–Briggs Type Indicator.* Palo Alto, California: Consulting Psychologists Press.

Nunnally, J. C. 1978. *Psychometric theory.* New York: McGraw-Hill.

Peters, T. J. & R. H. Waterman Jr 1982. *In search of excellence.* New York: Warner.

Pierce, G. R., I. G. Sarason, B. R. Sarason 1991. General and relationship-based perceptions of social support: are two constructs better than one? *Journal of Personality and Social Psychology* **61**, 1028–39.

Power, M. J., L. A. Champion, S. J. Aris 1988. The development of a measure of social support: the Significant Others (SOS) Scale. *British Journal of Clinical Psychology* **27**, 349–58.

Raskin, R. & C. S. Hall 1979. A Narcissistic Personality Inventory. *Psychological Reports* **45**, 590.

Raskin, R. & H. Terry 1988. A principal components analysis of the Narcissistic Personality Inventory and further evidence of its construct validity. *Journal of Personality and Social Psychology* **34**, 890–902.

Rogers, C. 1957. The necessary and sufficient conditions of therapeutic personality change. *Journal of Consulting Psychology* **21**, 95–103.

Rokeach, M. 1969. Value systems and religion. *Review of Religious Research* **11**, 2–23.

Rosenberg, M. 1965. *Society and the adolescent self-image*. Princeton, New Jersey: Princeton University Press.

Rotter, J. B. 1966. Generalized expectancies of internal versus external control of reinforcement. *Psychological Monographs* **80** (1, whole no. 609).

Royal Holloway University of London 1988. *Ethical Committee notes for guidance*. Egham, Surrey: Royal Holloway University of London.

Ryckman, R. M. 1993. *Theories of personality*. Pacific Grove, California: Brooks/Cole.

Scheffe, H. A. 1953. A method of judging all contrasts in the analysis of violence. *Biometrika* **40**, 87–104.

Selznick, G. & S. Steinberg 1969. *The tenacity of prejudice: anti-semitism in contemporary America*. New York: Harper & Row.

Siegel, S. & N. J. Castellan 1988. *Non-parametric statistics for the behavioural sciences*. New York: McGraw-Hill.

Smith, J. 1973. A quick measure of achievement motivation. *British Journal of Social and Clinical Psychology* **12**, 137–43.

Stark, R., D. B. Foster, C. Y. Glock, H. E. Quinley. 1971. *Wayward shepherds: prejudice and the protestant clergy*. New York: Harper & Row.

Swetland, R. C., D. J. Keyser, W. A. O'Connor 1983. *Tests*. Kansas City: Test Corporation of America.

Tabachnick, B. G. & L. S. Fidell 1989. *Using multivariate statistics*, 2nd edn. New York: HarperCollins.

Terman, L. M. & M. A. Merrill 1960. *Stanford-Binet Intelligence Scale*. New York: Houghton Mifflin.

Thurstone, L. L. 1931. The measurement of social attitudes. *Journal of Abnormal and Social Psychology* **26**, 249–69.

Trapp, A. & N. Hammond 1994. *The CTI directory of psychology software*. York: University of York CTI Centre for Psychology.

Truax, C. B. & R. R. Carkhuff 1967. *Toward effective counselling and psychotherapy*. Chicago: Aldine.

Wechsler, D. 1955. *The Wechsler Adult Intelligence Scale*. New York: Psychological Corporation.

West, R. 1991. *Computing for psychologists*. Chur, Switzerland: Harwood Academic Publishers.

Wilson, G. D. & J. R. Patterson 1968. A new measure of conservatism (C). *British Journal of Social and Clinical Psychology* **7**, 164–269.

Zigmond, A. S. & Snaith, R. P. 1983. The Hospital Anxiety and Depression Scale. *Acta Psychiatrica Scandinavica* **67**, 361–70.

Zuckerman, M. & B. Lubin 1963. *The Multiple Affect Adjective Check List*. San Diego, California: Edits.

Index